THE POWER OF KNOWLEDGE

HEMED

THE ISRAELI SCIENCE CORPS

URIEL BACHRACH

THE POWER OF KNOWLEDGE

HEMED

THE ISRAELI SCIENCE CORPS

URIEL BACHRACH

SAMUEL WACHTMAN'S SONS   DEKEL PUBLISHING HOUSE

THE POWER OF KNOWLEDGE
HEMED: THE ISRAELI SCIENCE CORPS

Uriel Bachrach
Copyright © 2016

Dekel Publishing House
www.dekelpublishing.com

North American rights by
Samuel Wachtman's Sons, Inc.
ISBN 978-1-888820-97-3

Editor:	Zvi Morik
Language editing:	Kathleen Roman
Proof reading:	Dory Morik

Open chapter fleuron images from @Truemitra - FreeVector.com
Molotov Cocktail © Kunertus / Dreamstime.com

Cover design and typesetting by

DESIGN PEAKS®

For information contact:

Dekel Publishing House	**Samuel Wachtman's Sons, Inc.**
P.O. Box 45094	2460 Garden Road, Suite C
Tel Aviv 6145002, Israel	Monterey, CA 93940, U.S.A.
Tel: +972 3506-3235	Tel: 831 649-0669
Fax: +972 3506-7332	Fax: 831 649-8007
Email: info@dekelpublishing.com	Email: samuelwachtman@gmail.com

*This book is devoted with love and respect
to my dear wife Zohara, who supported
and encouraged me during my work.*

*There was a little city, and few men within it; and there
came a great king against it, and besieged it, and built
great bulwarks against it. Now there was found in it a
poor wise man, and he by his wisdom delivered the city;
yet no man remembered that same poor man.*

From Ecclesiastes Chapter 9 verse 14.

TABLE OF CONTENTS

PREFACE

There is no doubt that the development of armaments has been and continues to be of great importance for the Israel Defense Forces (IDF). Guns, rifles, and hand grenades are developed to protect soldiers in the battlefield. Tanks are used to assist the infantry in combat. Battleships and submarines are designed to defend and attack at sea. Planes and missiles have strengthened the power of the Air Force. Sixty or seventy years ago, the importance of military research was questioned by Israeli scientists. Moreover, only a small number of scientists volunteered to serve in the Haganah.[1] Later, though, they were joined by a limited number of students from The Hebrew University of Jerusalem and the Technion in Haifa.

David Ben-Gurion was informed of this effort, gave his blessing to its activities, and suggested that their scope be broadened. In October 1947, a Scientific Department was established by the Haganah, and five months later, prior to Israel's declaration of independence, the chief of staff of the Haganah gave an official order to establish a Science Corps (referred to by the acronym HEMED in Hebrew). This Corps operated in four different locations: Jerusalem, Tel Aviv, Rehovot, and Haifa. At all of these bases, crucial research was conducted to support the defense of the newly established State.

---

1 The Haganah was a Jewish paramilitary organization in British Mandate Palestine that operated from 1920 to 1948.

Several years following the end of the War of Independence, HEMED was converted into EMET and in 1968, Rafael (the Armament Development Authority) was formed. Students who served in HEMED joined universities and research institutes and contributed much to the development of basic and applied sciences in Israel.

Uriel Bachrach was one of the students who joined the group, and he was later appointed professor of microbiology at The Hebrew University. In this book he describes the events related to the formation of HEMED, its accomplishments, and its contributions to the defense of the *Yishuv* (the Jewish community in Eretz Israel) before, during, and after the War of Independence. This book will enlighten readers regarding the vitally important contribution of HEMED to strengthening the various units of the IDF. I am certain readers will gain a wealth of new knowledge and an understanding of the role of this important story in the history of the IDF and of Israel.

I took an active part in the development of HEMED and was familiar with its activities. Even so, I was excited to read the stories documented in this book. Moreover, Uriel Bachrach describes the events in a reliable and a readable version.

I highly recommend that all those interested in studying the history of the research of defense in Israel read this book. It will provide them with many insights into the tremendous efforts that led to so many vitally important results.

אפרים קציר

Ephraim Katzir
Commander of HEMED (Lt. Colonel)
Fourth President of the State of Israel

INTRODUCTION

More than sixty years have elapsed since the State of Israel was created. During this time, a new generation has grown up. Its members did not participate in the struggle for independence and are not aware of the spirit that prevailed in the country prior to the declaration of independence. As time passes, I sense the importance of recording my memories of these times for the benefit of my grandchildren and their contemporaries.

One of the most fascinating chapters in the history of the State of Israel concerns the contribution of young Israeli scientists to the security of the newly established State. The term *Cheil Mada* (the Science Corps)—or HEMED, as it was known—remains largely unknown. Only a handful of members of today's generation are aware that David Ben-Gurion was instrumental in forming a corps (similar to the Naval Corps or Medical Corps) with its own military tag. This corps endeavored to overcome the embargo imposed on Israel and to strengthen the newly established State. The Science Corps was officially created in April 1948, and in 1952 it was transferred from the military authorities and recreated as a civilian body under the supervision of the Ministry of Defense.

I am fortunate to have in my possession documents from those days. While some of them have deteriorated over time, I have chosen to use them here in addition to describing my own experiences. I interviewed many of my comrades in order to verify the facts. I would like to note that this book is not intended to be a history book in the ordinary sense, but rather an attempt to convey the spirit that prevailed at the time the events describe here took place.

I would like to acknowledge the encouragement of my commanders, Ephraim Katzir and Uri Littauer. Nathan Sharon and Reuven Eshel added important information and clarified some of the events. My associates, Shaul Katz, Igal Talmi, Uzi Eilam, Alex Keynan, Moshe (Moja) Epstein, Uzi Sharon, Gabriella Fischer (widow of the late Ernst Fischer), Amos Chorev, Yossi Ben-Hanan, and many of my comrades played an important role in the consolidation of my ideas and contributed a great deal to the book.

On April 10, 2006, Nathan Sharon and I organized a meeting of the veterans of HEMED. This meeting was sponsored by the Israel Academy of Science and Humanities and chaired by Ephraim Katzir (1). The meeting was recorded and documented (free of charge) by Benny Uri. We all thank him for his important contribution.

Here my story begins.

CHAPTER 1:

MY ACTIVITY IN THE HAGANAH

A. Childhood and Sheikh Abreik[2]

I grew up in the town of Petach Tikvah and graduated from Moriah High School in Tel Aviv in the summer of 1944. Many of our teachers at Moriah subsequently fulfilled important functions at The Hebrew University of Jerusalem. Thus, Dr. Jacob Katz, who taught us history, became rector there, Y. Kutscher, who taught us Bible, was awarded the Israel Prize and became a professor of Hebrew language, and Dr. Yehoshua Blau, who also received the Israel Prize, became a professor of Arabic language. Most of my classmates were members of the Haganah, an underground movement controlled by the Jewish Agency, but a few students joined the Irgun (Etzel).[3] One of these was Ovadia Raziel, a relative of David Raziel, who was the commander of the Irgun. Our underground activities were somewhat routine. There was only one hero, Avraham Schwartz-

---

2   On the Galilee side of the narrow pass between the plain of Acre and Esdraelon, the village of **Sheikh Abreik** stands on a low hill. It was apparently the burial site of the biblical Barak, son of Avinoam.

3   The Irgun Tzvai Leumi (known as the Irgun or by its Hebrew acronym Etzel), was an armed Jewish underground organization in Palestine, commanded by Menachem Begin.

stein, who became the commander of Kibbutz Nitzanim and fell in battle when the Egyptian army attacked the kibbutz in 1948. During summer vacations, we volunteered to work in settlements, accompanied by one of our teachers (Picture 1). The work camp was in a religious youth village near Haifa. These were the days (1942) when Palestine was threatened by the advancing German army, commanded by Field Marshall Rommel, who was eventually defeated at the Battle of El Alamein.

Picture 1. The work camp (summer 1942)

Instructors from Kibbutz Yagur came to train us, so that in case of emergency, we could join fighters in the forests of Mount Carmel to defend Jewish settlements (like Tito's partisans in Yugoslavia).

In the summer of 1944, I graduated from high school and was ordered by the Haganah to be trained as a platoon commander in a course in Sheikh Abreik. For two months, we slept in tents. The food and sanitary conditions in the camp were very poor. We had no refrigerator and the "dining room" consisted of a tent, where we found bread and a barrel of oil (in lieu of butter or margarine). All of us suffered from diarrhea.

The home of Alexander Zaid,[4] located near our encampment, was used for physical training with the permission of Zippora, his widow (Picture 2). Weapons were concealed in an orchard near Sde Yaakov. There we were taught to shoot rifles and pistols by our instructors, commanders of the Haganah and the Palmach.[5]

Picture 2. Platoon commanders' course in Sheikh Abreik, summer 1944 (Zippora Zaid is in the center, wearing a white dress).

Most of the trainees in this course had grown up in Palestine, and there was also a group of new immigrants. Some

4   Alexander Zaid was one of the founders of the Hashomer organization, which was established in Kfar Tavor in the Lower Galilee in 1909 and served as the foundation for the establishment of other defense groups.

5   Palmach: The elite Jewish strike force of the Haganah prior to the establishment of the State of Israel. The volunteers combined military training with agricultural work in kibbutzim (communal farming villages).

of them were orphans who survived the Holocaust and came to Palestine via Teheran and were therefore called the Teheran Children. They taught us Russian songs and also one in Yiddish, which related the story of a boy selling cigarettes that were wet not because of raindrops, but because of tears. Dov Feit was one of these children, as was another new immigrant named Diamond, who was the commander of Kibbutz Kfar Darom in 1948. Dov fought in the Negev and at the Castel (a stronghold near Jerusalem). He received a medal for his courage and conduct in battle. Another of these children, Joseph Pomeranz, served in the army as a high-ranking officer. After finishing the course, we launched a night attack from our base to Mishmar Ha'emek (a twenty-mile march) and finished with a parade (Picture 3). We had to listen to a speech by Moshe Sneh (the chief of staff of the Haganah), and we were so exhausted that we all fell asleep as he spoke! All the graduates of this course fulfilled important functions as commanders during the War of Independence.

Picture 3. Parade of graduates of the platoon commanders' course in Mishmar Ha'emek (1944). The picture was intentionally blurred in order to prevent identification by the British Police.

B. Petach Tikvah

In the fall of 1944, I returned to Petach Tikvah and had to decide what to do next. I could join the Jewish Brigade of the British Army, serve in the Palmach, or be active in the Haganah in Petach Tikvah. Benjamin Gibli, who was in charge of the intelligence activities of the Haganah in our area, suggested that I join the British Police forces, to serve as a clerk, but also to act as a spy. I did not like this idea and instead decided to join the Jewish Settlement Police (Picture 4).

The Jewish Settlement Police (JSP) was part of the British Police force in Palestine, based on an agreement between the Jewish Agency and the British Police. Members of the JSP had their own uniforms and were supplied with guns (Italian carbines) taken from battle in the western desert. Members of the JSP belonged to the Haganah and used the weapons for training. Picture 4 depicts me in my British uniform, while Picture 5 shows a team of policemen.

Picture 4. The author in the uniform of the Jewish Settlement Police (1945)

Picture 5. A team of Jewish Settlement Policemen with a Lewis machine gun

At the beginning of each month, we were paid by the British authorities. British Sgt. Hobson came with his paymaster and gave £6 to each of us. The British regarded us as natives in one of their colonies. According to instructions, we had to receive the money with our left hand and salute with our right. The first time I was so confused (or thrilled) that I received the money with my right hand and saluted with the notes. The sergeant did not like it and shouted, "As you were," meaning that I should repeat the action. I eventually learned how to do this. We also had to polish our boots and iron our uniforms.

Bayonet fighting was also part of our training (Picture 6). During the War of Independence, on January 14, 1948, Aryeh Tepper's company attacked Chirbet Zacharia using bayonets (2). Apparently, Jewish volunteers from South Africa conducted a bayonet battle in Udga on January 3, 1949 (3). The nickname of Haim Bar-Lev (who served as IDF chief of staff in 1968) was "Kidoni" (bayonet), as he was wounded by a bayonet while training in the Palmach.

Picture 6. Bayonet training in Migdal Zedek (summer 1945)

In Petach Tikvah, I was appointed commander of a company in Regiment 19 of the Haganah. I also served as secretary of the regiment (concealing classified documents). In order to fulfill these functions, I was given a vehicle in the form of a rusty bicycle. I assume that I was appointed secretary of the regiment because my father was a physician and we had one of the rare telephones in Petach Tikvah.

During my service as a policeman, I participated in a reconnaissance-commanding course. We surveyed Arab villages near our neighborhood. In those days, we did not have cameras with which to take pictures of enemy "objects." Instead, we employed the techniques used by Gary Cooper in the film *For*

Whom the Bells Tolls and drew them (Picture 7). This was a bridge over the Yarkon River and was a strategic object, as a train passed over it.

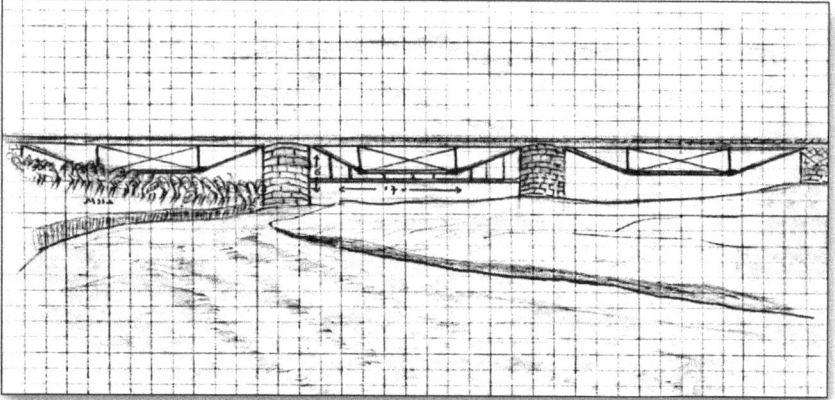

Picture 7. A drawing of a bridge over the Yarkon River (summer 1945)

Picture 8. Training my company at Kibbutz Givat Hashlosha (summer 1945)

In my company, I trained teenage boys and girls (Picture 8). I emphasized training for night combat, navigating by the stars, crawling, and hiding. I was told that this training saved the lives of many of these teenagers during the War of Independence. Additional training focused on man-to-man combat, physical exercises, and drills. The final stage of training included shooting (rifles and pistols) and throwing hand grenades. Marching was practiced during another phase of training, which included a march from the Mediterranean Sea to the Sea of Galilee (Picture 9).

Picture 9. A march to the Sea of Galilee (Arbel Canyon, summer 1945)

I also sailed on a boat from Tel Aviv to meet a ship carrying illegal immigrants (Picture 10). We failed to find the ship and spent the night near the ruins of the Crusader Castle of Atlit. We suspected that the ship was captured by British destroyers and that the illegal immigrants were brought to the port of Haifa and imprisoned there. As we sailed to Haifa, we found out that the port there was under curfew. I had a forged fisherman's certificate, but when I disembarked, I was arrested by an Arab policeman, who said in Arabic, "*Walla inte min albarbur*" (You are from the steam ship), but when I answered him in Arabic he realized that I was not an immigrant (still, he was not convinced by my fisherman's certificate). In the end, he let me go.

Picture 10. On the high sea (summer 1945)

During my service, I became a mounted policeman (Picture 11). I did not hesitate to ride a horse at night to surprise thieves and prevent crops being stolen from the fields of Tel Hashomer.

As a resident of Palestine, I held an identity card that attested to the fact that I was a real Palestinian (Picture 12). Palestine was part of the British Empire, so its residents automatically became British subjects.

Picture 11. A mounted policeman

Picture 12. The author is a real Palestinian

C. Jerusalem

In the fall of 1945, I began to study chemistry at The Hebrew University of Jerusalem (the only university in Palestine).

In Jerusalem, I also took an active part in the Haganah. Man-to-man combat training was conducted in one of the schools in the city, while the police station at the seminary in Beit Hak-erem served as a base for rifle training.

Here too, part of the training was marching. The march from Jerusalem to Masada was one of the most difficult ones we undertook. In the spring of 1946, I was among the approximately three hundred boys and girls who marched through the Judean Desert, carrying food, water, blankets, and sticks (Picture 13). We approached Masada from the west and descended the Snake Path to reach the Dead Sea (Picture 14).

Picture 13. The march through the Judean Desert (spring 1946)

Finally we camped at the oasis of Ein Gedi and used our blankets and sticks to build tents (Picture 15). As we rested there, Bedouins from the area began to attack us. They were armed with swords and daggers, while we had only sticks. There were rumors that some of the water canteens contained hand grenades, but I could never verify these.

Picture 14. The descent from Masada via the Snake Path, with the Dead Sea in the background. Two boys are standing on the slope to prevent their descending comrades from sliding.

Picture 15. The camp at Ein Gedi. Sticks and blankets were used to construct tents.

I had become friendly with a doctor who accompanied us and when the Bedouins started to bother us, he asked me to climb up a tree and to hang a white towel there. When the Bedouins asked in Arabic, "*Shu hada*?" (What is this?), I answered, also in Arabic, "*Hada mustashfa*" (This is a hospital.) Soon afterward four Bedouins carried a patient to our "hospital." The doctor examined him and gave him an aspirin tablet. He then informed the patient that he must drink two cups of water and rest in his tent for two days, adding that this was very strong medicine and that four strong men should watch him and prevent him from getting up. After a while, many patients were sent to their tents. We were very relieved. In lieu of payment, our helpful doctor received dates and other fruits from his patients and their families.

Picture 16. Sailing on the Dead Sea from Sodom on boats carrying potassium chloride (I am standing on the boat, marked with an arrow).

Some of our comrades slipped and injured their legs. We had to send a message to Jerusalem to request assistance. We had no radio and the only means of communication we had were pigeons, which we had brought with us from Jerusalem. Unfortunately, we had ignored the fact that there are many birds of prey in the Judean Desert. Our pigeons never arrived at their Jerusalem destination. Notably, at the end of the 1940s, Y. Wilensky from Kibbutz Ma'aleh Hachamisha introduced the use of pigeons for communication purposes. He organized his pigeons as a military unit and kept records concerning flight times, ranges, and number of messages delivered. Using the pigeons as messengers, he maintained contact between his kibbutz and the settlements in Gush Etzion. Later, the army formed a special pigeon unit as part of the Signal Corps (4).

In those days, there was no road along the coast of the Dead Sea and we had to climb the rocky hills toward Jericho. We found it difficult, as we had some boys with broken limbs. Boats were sailing from Sodom from the southern part of the Dead Sea to the north carrying potassium chloride. We stood at the shore of the sea, waving blankets, trying, like Robinson Crusoe, to attract the attention of the sailors. This method failed, but they did notice the bonfires we lit. We climbed onto the boats (Picture 16) and, after many adventures, finally returned to Jerusalem.

One of the duties assigned to the youth brigades of the Haganah was posting illegal placards for the Haganah. In Jerusalem, this activity was dangerous, and the boys and girls involved in it risked being arrested or even shot by British policemen or detectives from the CID (Criminal Investigation Department). Alexander Rubovitch, a sixteen-year-old boy, was arrested and killed by British policemen for this offense.

Yehoshua Arieli recalls:

In darkness, they left their homes and went to a predetermined destination. There, they received a bucket filled with glue and a package of illegal posters. Usually, they were a "romantic couple," a boy and a girl. One of them came to a wall and rubbed the glue on it, while the other attached the document on the glue-coated wall. Occasionally, there was a third teenager whose function was to warn the couple if any policeman approached (5, translated from the Hebrew).

Gideon. Lahav adds:

We met on Rabbi Kook Street at the Patt Bakery, otherwise known as the "Institute." From there, the couples started on their mission, posting the illegal posters. Often, we tried to improve the techniques we used for the preparation of the posters. Uriel Bachrach, a student of chemistry, was active in this respect. Grizim (commander of the Modi'im Battalion) told him: "The most major problem is the glue. The British policemen use the glue on the hands of the arrested teenagers as evidence in court. You have to solve this problem!" Bachrach organized a laboratory at the "Institute," tried using starch as glue, and finally suggested spreading the glue on the poster, so that only one youngster was needed for the action, which could be carried out rapidly and without leaving traces on his hands (6, translated from the Hebrew).

And so, devising this new method of gluing Haganah posters to walls provided me with my first experience in research and development.

Field-training with guns was carried out in kibbutzim near Jerusalem (Ramat Rachel, Ma'aleh Hachamisha, and Kiryat Anavim). There was also a special training area called "Our Home" near a hill called "Wind Mountain," west of Jerusalem. While training there on June 29, 1946, we awakened to the sight of British armored cars approaching Ma'aleh Hachamisha and Kiryat Anavim. We immediately packed our belongings (including the tents) and rushed back toward Jerusalem. This was the so-called "Black Sabbath," when many Jewish leaders (including members of the Jewish Agency) were arrested and imprisoned by the British government in a camp near Latrun.

CHAPTER 2:

STUDYING CHEMISTRY AT
THE HEBREW UNIVERSITY

As mentioned above, in the fall of 1945, I began my chemistry studies at The Hebrew University. We were a group of some twenty students. Among us, there were ex-servicemen from the British armed forces (Y. Lipschitz, Romek Fein, and Adam Schatkai, who was an RAF pilot). In addition, there were ex-servicemen from the Palmach (reservists Nathan Sharon and Daniel Reich) and active members of the Haganah. There was also a deaf student called Emmanuel Goldschlag-Meron. He liked to test explosives, as he could feel the shock waves. He taught us that we could produce explosives by mixing crystals of iodine with ammonia. His hands and face were full of scars, but his experience with explosives helped us during the War of Independence.

During the first and second years, the studies were boring. During the first year, we were required to conduct qualitative chemical analyses. Under the supervision of Prof. Kirson, we had to separate strontium and barium derivatives. During the second year, we had to determine the quantity of lead in glass samples. This was a difficult task; first we had to crush the glass sample in a mortar, taking care not to get glass particles in our eyes. Obviously, one could not sneeze during the first steps of the analyses. Today we know that such analyses can be carried out in several minutes using atomic absorbance technologies.

The third year of our studies was more interesting. Prof. Moshe Weizmann taught us organic chemistry. He resembled his brother, Chaim Weizmann, and constantly told us, "This world is full of miracles, *kinderlach* ["children" in Yiddish]. My brother is a good chemist [he invented a method to produce acetone from starch, a process that helped the United Kingdom during the First World War], and they made a politician out of him. I am a good politician, but I have to teach chemistry." In those days, The Hebrew University had only eight hundred students and most of the examinations were oral. If a student had to be examined by Moshe Weizmann, the first question was always "Can you play chess?" If you played well you must be intelligent and obviously you knew organic chemistry. He told us stories about his studies in the department of Prof. Rozsiska (a Nobel Prize laureate) in Switzerland. One Friday, he stopped his lectures and said: "*Kinderlach,* today is Sabbath eve. Go and play with the girls." Those who had girlfriends rushed away and those who did not began an intensive search for one!

CHAPTER 3:

THE WAR OF INDEPENDENCE

A. Preparations for a Struggle

In September 1947 (before the United Nations voted on the resolution to partition Palestine), it was clear that war would soon break out. It was, therefore, decided that a number of Haganah commanders would be sent to Kfar Etzion for advanced training under the command of Mosh Silberschmidt, who taught us how to handle a Sten submachine gun (our own product), fire a mortar, and prepare Molotov cocktails (Picture 17). Silberschmidt fell in battle during the War of Independence with the rank of major.

Picture 17. Molotov cocktail

We were also trained to attack fortified positions. We lay on barbed wire while our comrades stepped on us. We attached explosives to the doors of fortified positions and learned to spray pepper on our tracks to prevent British police dogs from tracing us. Finally, we returned to Jerusalem to await orders.

On November 29, 1947, the United Nations passed a resolution that adopted the plan for the partition of Palestine. We all danced in the streets of Jerusalem, celebrating this historic event. On December 2, 1947, I was busy in the chemical laboratory at The Hebrew University, working with my classmate Daniel Reich, who would fall two months later with the Convoy of Thirty-Five on the way to Kfar Etzion. Rumors spread that the war had started and indeed we saw smoke and flames near the Jaffa Gate in the Jewish commercial center. Another rumor spread that Haganah commanders should assemble at the Trade Union House (Beit Hahistadrut). There I met with many of my friends. Pistols were recovered from their hiding places and distributed to us. We were warned not to keep intact guns in our possession, as we could be searched by British policemen; guns were dismantled and carried in separate parts by two people. One carried bullets, the other the barrel, and we were instructed, if searched by a policeman, to say that we had found this "unknown object" in the street and were on our way to the police station to hand it over. We walked in the direction of the commercial center and on Princess Mary Street near Studio Theater, there was a roadblock and we were stopped. Among the policemen, there was a Jewish officer named Langer (who was a member of the Haganah). He saw our bulging pockets and told the other policemen that he knew us and that we were on our way to Yemin Moshe (near the commercial center), so they let us go. At the same time, a member of the Irgun approached the roadblock and unfortunately a pistol was seen stuck in his belt. The British policemen approached him and said, "In the name of His Majesty, you are arrested." The youngster yelled at him, "Do not be a fool, I will kill you!" The policeman was shocked and shouted, "Go!" We went down to the commercial center and saw a mob coming from the Jaffa Gate (Picture 18), looting and burning shops (Picture 19). After an exchange of fire, the looters retreated (Picture 20).

Picture 18. The mob streaming from the Jaffa Gate

Picture 19. The commercial center in flames

Picture 20. The retreating looters

After completing our operation, we were ordered to move to the teachers' seminary in Beit Hakerem. There we slept on the floor of the gymnasium and generous women supplied us with food. On the following day, commanders of various units came to the seminary to select candidates to serve with them. Suddenly, I saw Mosh Silberschmidt, whom I knew from the course in Kfar Etzion. He invited me to join the Department of Operations of the District of Jerusalem, under his command. On December 8, 1947, I moved to the basement of Biermann's House on Itamar Ben-Avi Street and started to plan operations. Trude Dotan, a renowned archeologist who studied the history of the Philistines, was a member of our team. The village of Silwan (on the slope of the Mount of Olives), was our first objective (Picture 21). We received the information from fighters of the Arab Department of the Palmach. One of them was a fellow called Salach, who was dressed like an Arab and did not take a shower for weeks. We also received photos taken by pilots of the so-called "Air Service," from which the Israeli Air Force was created after Israel declared independence.

Picture 21. A picture of the village of Silwan (taken by one of our secret agents)

B. The War Begins

On January 16, 1948, a company of thirty-five fighters left Har-Tuv to reinforce the besieged settlements of Gush Etzion. An Arab shepherd detected the fighters and recruited armed Arabs from the neighboring villages. During the fierce battle that ensued, all thirty-five of the fighters were killed. Many of them were students at The Hebrew University. One of them was my classmate Daniel Reich, the only child of Carl Reich, professor of zoology at The Hebrew University. At this point, my conscience began to bother me, and I could not bear the idea that I was sitting in an office while others were struggling in the battlefields.

I discussed the matter with Mosh Silberschmidt and asked to be transferred to a combat unit. I reminded Silberschmidt that I had graduated from a reconnaissance-commanders course. On February 22, the brigade commander, Dror, sent the following message (see Picture 22) to Avrashka Tamir, commander of Company B of the Jerusalem Brigade (he later became a general):

> *22-1-48*
>
> *To: Avrashka*
>
> *From: Dror*
>
> *Upon your request, I transfer to you the reconnaissance commander. Please attach him to your commanding staff unit.* [translated from the Hebrew]

At the time, all orders were given in writing, using underground code names, as British forces left Palestine only four months later.

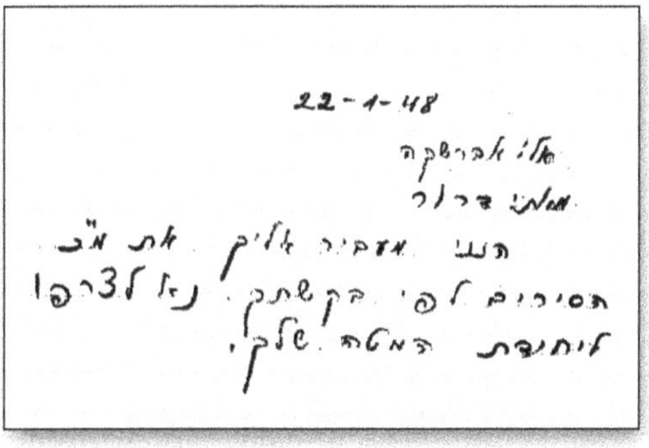
22-1-48
אל: אברשקה
מאת: דרור
הנני מעביר אליך את מ"כ
הסיור לפי בקשתך. נא לצרפו
ליחידת המטה שלך.

Picture 22. My transfer to Avrashka Tamir's unit

The King family home in Talpiot served as the headquarters of Company B. As I was attached to the headquarters of the company, I operated from there. Tamir appointed me commander of a platoon. The soldiers came from Tel Aviv (there were not enough soldiers in the Jerusalem area) and were not acquainted with the hilly Judean terrain. I began to train them for nighttime operations.

Several days later, Tamir ordered me to go to the Theodosius Monastery in the Judean Desert and find out whether volunteers from Serbia were training Palestinian gangs there. I was convinced that my soldiers were not trained for a long-range march in the desert and suggested we start with a more "minor operation." He agreed that we should inspect a hill north of Bethlehem, near Kibbutz Ramat Rachel. There was a wall around the hill, and therefore I marked the hill on my map as the "Walled Hill" ("Har Choma" in Hebrew). Today the official name of that hill is Walled Mountain. On January 28, 1948, we inspected the hill, found it empty, and mined it.

I needed more maps, so Tamir sent the following handwritten note (see Picture 23) to the Department of Operations:

To: The Department of Operations 24/1/48
From: Commander of Company B

Please give Uri all necessary assistance. I need more material so I can plan future operations against "objectives." Dror attached this reconnaissance officer to my company and promised to supply him with information, if needed.

Avrashka
Commander, Company B [translated from the Hebrew].

On January 26, 1948, I was ordered by Tamir to attack a convoy of armed Palestinians who were on their way from Hebron to Jerusalem. I immediately alerted my soldiers and we marched to a hill near Rachel's tomb. From our position, we could see the convoy approaching us (Picture 24). We fired at the first vehicle, which was hit, and its driver lost control. After some time, the Palestinians realized what had happened and launched a counterattack. I had a Sten submachine gun[6] (Picture 25) and tried to shoot at one of the attackers who approached me. I was terrified. My gun failed to shoot, apparently because the bullets were rusty. Fortunately, one of our fighters shot at the attackers, saving my life.

---

6   Sten gun: a British 9-mm submachine gun used extensively by British Commonwealth forces during World War II.

Picture 23. Avrashka Tamir's request

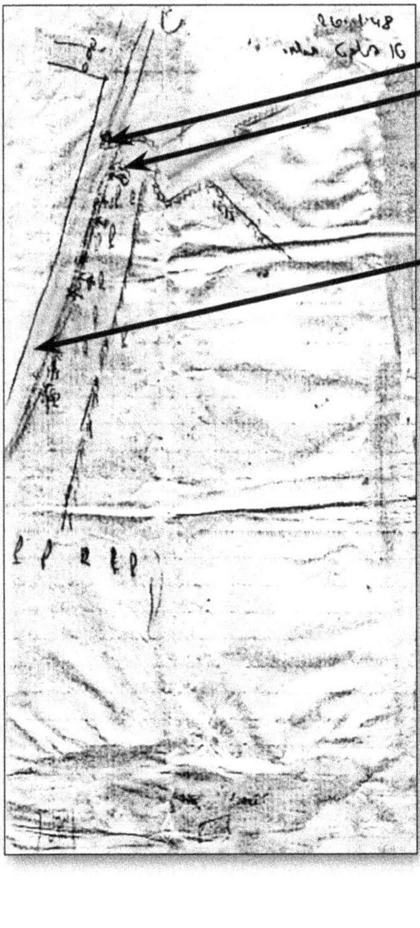

Machine gun
Land mine

Soldiers

Picture 24. Map of the ambush

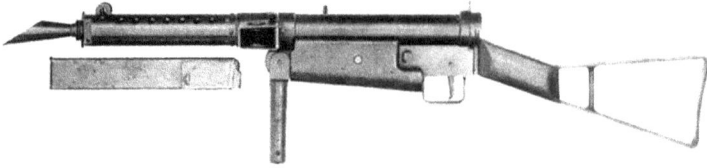

Picture 25. A Sten gun

Several years later, I traveled to Paris and met with some Israelis. A bearded fellow approached me and asked, "Are you The Chemist [my code name in Talpiot]?" He added: "I am Benjamin, who saved your life in the ambush in 1948. Now do me a favor, and tell my French wife that I fought in Jerusalem during the War of Independence." How could I refuse?

CHAPTER 4:

MILITARY SCIENTIFIC RESEARCH BEFORE
THE ESTABLISHMENT OF THE STATE

A. The Course on Mount Scopus

On February 1, 1948, I was ordered to report for a secret mission at the Hebrew High School (*HaGymnasia HaIvrit*) in Jerusalem. Upon arriving, I met some of my classmates from The Hebrew University, but we had no idea of the reason for our gathering. Finally, Dr. Aharon Katchalsky (later called Katzir) appeared and delivered the following speech to us:

Our nation is facing a dangerous situation. On May 15, British forces and administration will leave this country. Arab armies from neighboring countries will invade us. We do not have arms or military industries and the Western nations have imposed an embargo upon us. It is your duty to save our nation. [...] You are students and are open- minded. If I had selected chemists who were involved in the production of black boot polish, their entire outlook would be focused on black boot polish. Neither you nor I have ever been exposed to studies on chemical warfare. Tomorrow, I want to see you at the campus of

The Hebrew University, on Mount Scopus, to start your studies. Good luck! [translated from the Hebrew]

On the following day, February 2, 1948, some twenty students began their activities on Mount Scopus. This was the beginning of HEMED (the Science Corps). However, it should be recalled that earlier, Aharon Katchalsky had "recruited" some pioneers from the Haganah and the Palmach to "play" with explosives. They were aided by Elik Sochazewer, who was the head of the mechanical workshop of The Hebrew University and a graduate of the Polytechnic School in Warsaw. Sochazewer traveled around the world and collected books related to military technologies. When he was the head of the mechanical workshop at The Hebrew University, he became one of the founders of Israel Military Industries (Taas) in Jerusalem and contributed much to the armed forces during the early phases of the War of Independence.

We had never studied military chemistry, so we had to learn this subject. In the library of the Institute of Chemistry, we found a book titled *Chemicals in War* by A.M. Prentis. We studied the material described in the book and learned something about the field.

We remained on Mount Scopus for three weeks. During that time we dealt with explosives, incendiaries, smoke, and gases. The fact that we were students was very helpful in this respect, since we did not hesitate to discuss and study subjects that were new to us. One week was devoted to each subject. In the mornings, we dealt with theoretical aspects, each of us leading a seminar describing what he had learned from the book. In the afternoons, we turned to the practical aspects, synthesizing in the chemical laboratory the materials we had discussed theoretically in the mornings. For example, if in the morning we discussed the properties of TNT, in the afternoon we produced it. We conducted the seminars and the practical work without any instructor (luckily without any accidents during the production of the explosives). The only senior scientist who was with us was Alon Feldman-Radler-Talmi, a physical chemist, who later became head of the Department of Chemistry at Tel Aviv University. He knew something about explosives and taught us how to attach a detonator to a cord. A black delay cord one centimeter in length caused a one-second delay of the explosion. A yellow cord caused an explosion with no delay. Feldman-Radler-Talmi told us that during combat we would not have any tools to help us attach the cords, so we would have to place the detonators in our mouths and use our teeth to attach them. We did it. Even now, I do not understand how we were spared, and how no detonator exploded when we attached it with our teeth. After several months, Feldman-Radler-Talmi was sent to France to recruit scientists and armaments.

At that time, I was ordered to train the members of our group in throwing hand grenades. I was instructed to throw the hand grenades only outside the building and not to damage the marble plates that covered the entrance of the buildings. After this training, we joined the guards protecting Mount Scopus and at night, after finishing our chemical training, we protected the buildings. In light of these activities, we received a special medal engraved with the words "Protectors of the Mountain."

Prof. A. Shulov was the founder of the Biblical Zoo, which was at that time located on Mount Scopus. The roars of the lions frightened the Palestinians and they did not attack the campus. He described our activities thus:

> There were two groups who helped us to protect the mount. One group consisted of settlers from the villages of Atarot and Neveh Yaakov, who were evacuated from their homes. The second group consisted of students and junior scientists from The Hebrew University, who were active in the newly formed HEMED (the Science Corps). The two groups became part of the guards protecting the mount and contributed much to security during the

difficult times when we were isolated and cut off from the city of Jerusalem (7, translated from the Hebrew).

Aviva Kushnir, the widow of Tuvia Kushnir (a botanist who was killed with the thirty-five fighters on their way to Kfar Etzion), was with us on Mount Scopus. She had a dream in which her late husband ordered her to go back to the Palestinian village of Isawiya and retrieve from their garden the rare bulbs of the black tulip, which he had found on Mount Gilboa. She was determined to go, and it was difficult for us to convince her not to risk her life.

On March 28, 1948, Aharon Katchalsky wrote the following to his brother Ephraim, who was still in the United States:

> Several days after the beginning of the war, I enlisted a group of twenty students who studied military chemistry. Subsequently, more students of chemistry joined them, as did students of physics. All of these students contributed much to the security of the nation. Several weeks ago the commanders in chief declared that they would be recognized as a company in the Science Corps, HEMED. (8)

It should be remembered that at that time, supplies of military equipment, guns, ammunition, and explosives were very limited. At the end of year 1947 (several months before the outbreak of the war), Shlomo Gur was asked by the commanders of the Haganah to reveal the numbers of active members of the Haganah and their equipment. He summarized as follows:

> The Palmach had 2,000 boys and girls in full active service and another 1,000 in the "reserve" units. Despite many attempts to supply these soldiers with arms, the Palmach had only 700 English rifles, 10 three-inch mortars, 30 two-inch mortars, (all produced by us), 40 Bren ma-

chine guns, 10 French machine guns (Chateaux), 80 pistols, 354 submachine guns, and 3,384 hand grenades (not listed). (9)

Obviously, these arms did not cover the needs of the elite Haganah fighting force.

WEAPON (December 1947)		
	HAGANAH	**PALMACH**
Rifles	10,000	700
Mortars 2" *	972	30
" 3"	96	10
Machine guns	444	40+10
Submachine guns **	1,900	
Pistols	3,830	80
Hand grenades *	53,000	
Number of Soldiers 3	**30,000**	**2,000+1,000**
* U.S.A ** T.M.T		

The other (non-Palmach) members of the Haganah had 10,000 rifles and 3,830 pistols. Again, this equipment could not cover the needs of more than thirty thousand Haganah members. There was also a serious shortage of explosives. The amount of TNT was limited and the Palmach fighters had to use a primitive explosive, cheddite, to blow up bridges over the Jordan River. Cheddite was first produced in Haute-Savoie, France, in the nineteenth century. It contained potassium chlorate and organic compounds such as paraffin or colophonium obtained from tree resins. Cheddite was less active than TNT and exploded when it was hit by rifle bullets.

On May 31, 1948, Ernst David Bergmann wrote to Chaim Weizmann:

> Our situation reminds me of London during the Blitz. The British were not prepared for the war, yet they won it. The comparison with the British Empire is flattering. […] We have to remember that we can trust nobody, only ourselves (10, translated from the Hebrew).

Ben-Gurion accepted this view and was determined to develop, research, and produce armaments by our own means and not rely on foreign sources.

B. First Steps

Even prior to the formation of HEMED, several weapons had been produced by a fledgling military industry in Eretz Israel. Thus, as early as the 1930s, three-inch mortars were produced, along with hand grenades (known as the "Polish" and the "Rubbing"). According to Ephraim Katzir:

> Even before the beginning of the War of Independence, some scientists from the Technion in Haifa, The Hebrew University of Jerusalem, and the Sieff Institute in Rehovot suggested that research in the disciplines of chemistry, physics, and engineering could assist members of the Haganah. These scientists could design new weapons and repair the existing ones. They could also acquaint themselves with the armaments of our enemies. Contact between scientists and the Israel Defense Forces stimulated joint activities. The fact that some of our scientists had participated in the research and development of armaments in World War II encouraged the formation of

HEMED, the Science Corps. At first, this unit was part of the Haganah, but after the establishment of the State of Israel, it became part of the Israel Defense Forces (11, translated from the Hebrew).

Amos Chorev, who was later promoted to the rank of general and became president of the Technion, was active in field trials of the newly produced weapons. He recalls (12):

I was the commander of Company H of the Palmach and we were active in the Judean Hills near Jerusalem. I was interested in explosives and especially in hollow charges[7] [Picture 26].

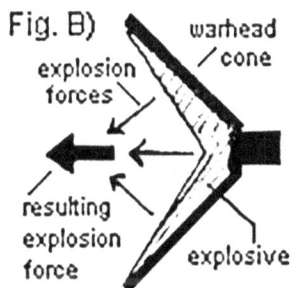

Picture 26. Hollow charge

In 1946 I was given a sample of a hollow-charged shell, produced by our industry by Aharon Donagi and Meir Rabinovitz. I started field experiments on the shores of the isolated Dead Sea and tested time bombs, thermites,[8] and incendiary bombs that contained metal powders and metal oxides.

---

7   A hollow charge is an arrangement of explosives around a conical or half-spherical metal insert, which is particularly suitable for piercing armor. It is used accordingly in tank ammunition, anti-tank weapons, and bombs.

8   Thermite is a pyrotechnic composition of a metal powder and a metal oxide. The reaction is used for thermite welding, often to join rail tracks.

When these materials were not supplied by the industry, we used the chemical laboratory of Prof. Moshe Weizmann (brother of Chaim Weizmann) at the university on Mount Scopus. He gave us his permission but was alarmed when a fire broke out during our experiments. [translated from the Hebrew]

During the course on Mount Scopus, we were trained to act as individuals. We were supposed to serve in different parts of the country, to start new industries, and to improve existing plants. At that time (the beginning of 1948), the British still controlled Palestine and the Criminal Investigation Department of the police was very active. HEMED had an office on Ben Yehuda Street in the center of Jerusalem. On the door of that office there was a sign that read "Onn Company." This was the code name of Aharon Katchalsky, who was the commander of the unit at that time (Picture 27).

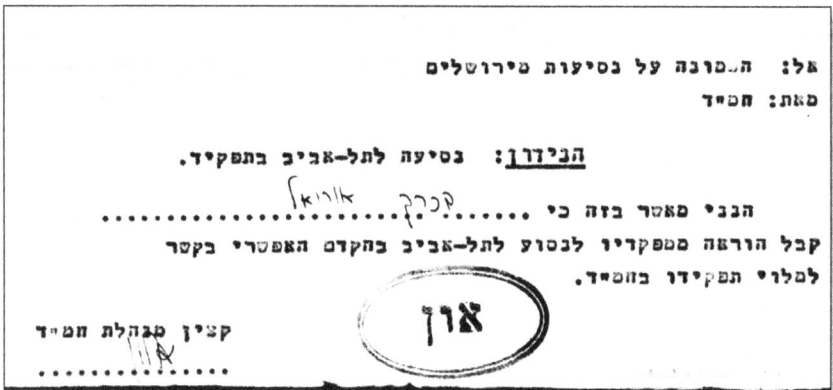

Picture 27. The "Onn" stamp appears on a document signed by Alon Feldman-Radler-Talmi.

The secretary of Onn Company was Ora Herzog (wife of Haim Herzog, who later became the president of the State of Israel). Only selected candidates were permitted to join this "company." The document in Picture 28 states that Ora Herzog left HEMED on March 15, 1948, and was replaced by Arieh Hurvitz ("Tzur").

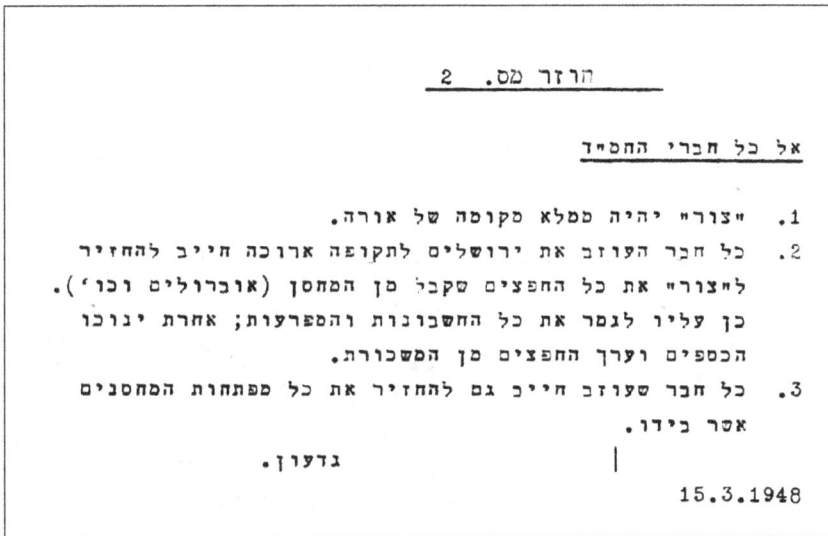

הרזר מס.   2

אל כל חברי החמ״ד

1.   "צורי" יהיה ממלא מקומה של אורה.
2.   כל חבר העוזב את ירושלים לתקופה ארוכה חייב להחזיר
     ל"צורי" את כל החפצים שקבל מן המחסן (אוברולים וכו')
     כן עליו לגמור את כל החשבונות והספרעות; אחרת ינוכו
     הכספים וערך החפצים מן המשכורת.
3.   כל חבר שעוזב חייב גם להחזיר את כל מפתחות המחסנים
     אשר בידו.
                                   גדעון.

                                          15.3.1948

Picture 28. Ora Herzog leaves HEMED and is replaced by "Tzur."

Onn Company was regarded as a secret, underground unit, so we could not use our real names. Thus, Uri Littauer was "Orli," Nathan Sharon was named "Natasha," Shimon Gatt (Grunwald) became "Shamgar," and I was named "Avishai."

In early 1948, the secretarial office was quite basic. Orders and communications were handwritten by members of the administration. An example of such a communication is depicted in Picture 29. This unique document was sent by Gideon Blauer to Mr. Battish, the owner of a pharmacy on Strauss Street in the center of Jerusalem. In this document (dated March 23, 1948), the owner of the drugstore was asked to supply the needed chemicals, with the hope that he would be paid after the establishment of the State. This is remarkable and demonstrates the degree to which people were ready to help one another and believed that they would be repaid whenever possible.

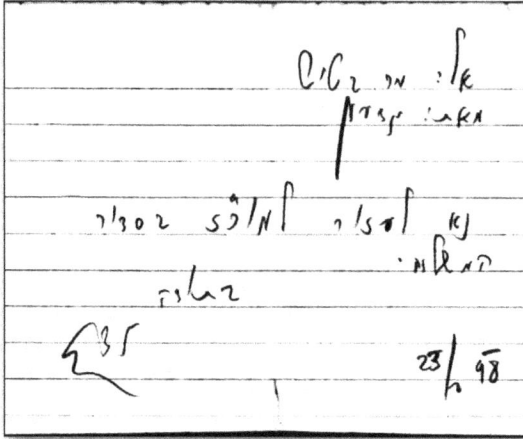

Picture 29. A communication from Gideon Blauer to drugstore owner Mr. Battish, with a request to supply chemicals with the hope that payment would be made when possible.

At the end of March 1948, Gideon Blauer was appointed administrator of Onn Company. He published the following rules :

Circular No. 1

1. Finances

a. All payments must be approved by Ora [Herzog].

b. Only heads of research groups can ask for support.

c. Meals will be supplied by the university restaurant upon showing a voucher. These can be obtained from "Tzur" in his office between 11:30 and 13:00.

2. Chemicals and materials

a. Information concerning the cost of materials can be obtained from "Tzur" in his office between 11:30 and 13:00.

3. Transportation

a. Transportation from workshops must be approved by "Tzur." [translated from the Hebrew]

Gideon Blauer, who signed this document, was born in Vienna in 1922. He immigrated to Palestine, studied chemistry at The Hebrew University, and received his M.Sc. degree in 1946. In 1947, Aharon Katchalsky asked him to join a group that dealt with military chemistry. In mid-1948, Blauer left Jerusalem, joined research groups on HEMED Base No. 1 (*Givah*, the "Hill"), and worked on flame throwers[9] and delay bombs (13).

After completing the course on Mount Scopus, we moved to the center of Jerusalem. We did not have uniforms and we all lived in our previous homes. Meals were supplied by a restaurant in Romema (a neighborhood in western Jerusalem). In March 1948, Jerusalem was already besieged, and food supplies were limited. So we were reduced to eating *hubeiza* (mallow).[10]

New members joined our "company" and we began to train them. At that time, we already had smoke hand grenades, which were produced by the industry. Colors could be added to the chemicals to serve as markers. These were used as signals for primitive planes, which dropped ammunition and supplies to isolated settlements.

We also had tear gas hand grenades, which contained chloroacetophenone. Experiments with tear gas had already started in the 1930s in Kibbutz Kiryat Anavim, in the Judean Hills, west of Jerusalem. In 1948, the industry produced large quantities of smoke and tear gas hand grenades.

---

9 A flamethrower or flame projector was a weapon that fired a burning stream of liquid. They were useful in close-quarters combat and attacks against tanks and fortifications.

10 *Hubeiza* is the Arabic word for the wild, edible mallow plant. Jerusalemites ate it while under siege during the War of Independence.

Tear gas was used even earlier. One day in the 1940s, Yitzhak Navon (who became the fifth president of the State of Israel) was summoned by his commander in the Haganah, Ephraim Katchalsky (who later became the fourth president of the State of Israel) to come to his home in Jerusalem.

Katchalsky gave him two test tubes containing tear gas. Navon was instructed to go to the Edison Theater, where a meeting of the Palestinian Communist Party was taking place. He was ordered to enter the theater and break the test tube to deter the participants. He entered through one of the doors and stepped on the test tube as he was instructed to do. After smelling the odor of the tear gas, he repeated the same action, entering by the second door. When he turned around to try to leave the theater, he was stopped by a British policeman who said: "This man stinks awfully! Search him!" The other policeman did what he was ordered to do, but he found nothing, not even the cotton wool that had been used to wrap the test tubes (14). It is amazing what future presidents can do!

C. My First Research and Development Activities in HEMED

Upon completing the course on Mount Scopus, I was sent on March 23, 1948, to an advanced course on mining and demolition that took place in "the Valley of Zion," the site at which the Givat Ram University campus was later constructed. I was the only member of HEMED who was sent to that course, which provided me with advanced training in mining and demolition. In the picture below (Picture 30), it is possible to see that we did not have military uniforms, and each of us came with his own clothing.

Picture 30. Demolition course, March 1948

After completing the course and becoming an expert on mining and demolition, I was ordered to produce fuses for time bombs. We were trained to work as individuals and to solve all problems without additional help. My first problem was to find a site for a "laboratory." After looking for a place, I found a ruin in a street now called Wallenberg Street (Picture 31). Raoul Wallenberg was a Swedish humanitarian who worked in Budapest, Hungary, during World War II and rescued Jews from the Germans. The ruin, located near the Bikur Cholim Hospital, had an interesting history. It was the site of the German Consulate and was decorated with the German flag. When World War II broke out, the building was confiscated by the British Police and became the headquarters of the Criminal Investigation Department, which arrested members of the Irgun. In revenge, the Irgun attacked the building and demolished it. So it was that this ruin became my "laboratory." Obviously, neither electricity nor running water was available there. Gideon Blauer contacted Meir Tobiansky, head of the

Jerusalem Electric Company, and asked for his help. Ironically, Meir Tobiansky, who was a Haganah commander, was wrongly suspected of collaborating with the British and executed in 1948 by the first military court. A year after the execution, Tobiansky was exonerated of all charges.

Picture 31. The ruin on Wallenberg Street that served as my first "laboratory."

The problem of electricity was solved, but I faced two additional problems. The first was where to find the chemicals needed for the fuses, and the second was which mechanical workshop could help me. Battish supplied the chemicals from his pharmacy (see Picture 29), with the promise that he would be paid by the future government of Israel. The mechanical parts were supplied by Elik Sochazewer, who, in addition to heading the mechanical workshop of The Hebrew University, had a private plant in the Tel Arza quarter in northern Jerusalem. After all these difficulties were overcome, fuses were prepared and delivered to the combat units.

D. The Involvement of HEMED in the Battles of Jerusalem

1. The Convoy from Kfar Etzion

The commanders of Kfar Etzion sent an urgent message to the chief of staff, demanding supplies, weapons, and the replacement of the so-called "student company" with new recruits. A well-equipped convoy was therefore sent from Jerusalem to isolated Kfar Etzion on Saturday, March 25, 1948. The Sabbath was selected because on this day there was no public transportation and buses were available for our use. In addition, the Sabbath was not a working day, so vehicles and drivers were not occupied.

Zvi Zamir, the commander of Battalion 6 of the Palmach, was in charge of the convoy, which contained thirty-five trucks and twelve armored cars. (Zamir went on to become a major general in the Israel Defense Forces and head of the Mossad.[11]) The convoy was supposed to leave at 4:00 a.m., but it was delayed and was ready only at 8:00. Yitzhak Navon, who was in charge of Intelligence Services in Jerusalem, listened to Palestinian communications and recommended we wait for another day.

His recommendation was not accepted and the convoy left Jerusalem on Saturday morning and arrived at Kfar Etzion. The convoy was supposed to return to Jerusalem after thirty minutes. This did not happen. It took more than two hours to load a damaged airplane onto one of the trucks. At that time, the Haganah had a rudimentary Air Service, manned by pilots from RAF and the United States Army Air Corps. A Piper aircraft belonging to that service was sent to check the

---

11 Mossad: The Institute for Intelligence and Special Operations

conditions of the road leading to Jerusalem. The pilot reported that many Arabs were gathering, blocking the road with rocks, and waiting for the convoy. Zamir believed that his convoy, four kilometers long, would be able to overcome the difficulties and return to Jerusalem. The convoy came to a small village called El-Khader, near Nebi Daniel, where it was stopped by armed Arabs. Seven trucks, four armored cars, and Zamir succeeded in returning to Kfar Etzion. Aryeh Tepper took command and ordered all his soldiers to leave the trucks and move to a building at the side of the road. The wounded were treated and the remaining soldiers exchanged fire with the attacking Arabs. They soon realized that they were running out of ammunition and asked for help. Reinforcements left Jerusalem but were not able to reach the besieged soldiers in Nebi Daniel (Picture 32).

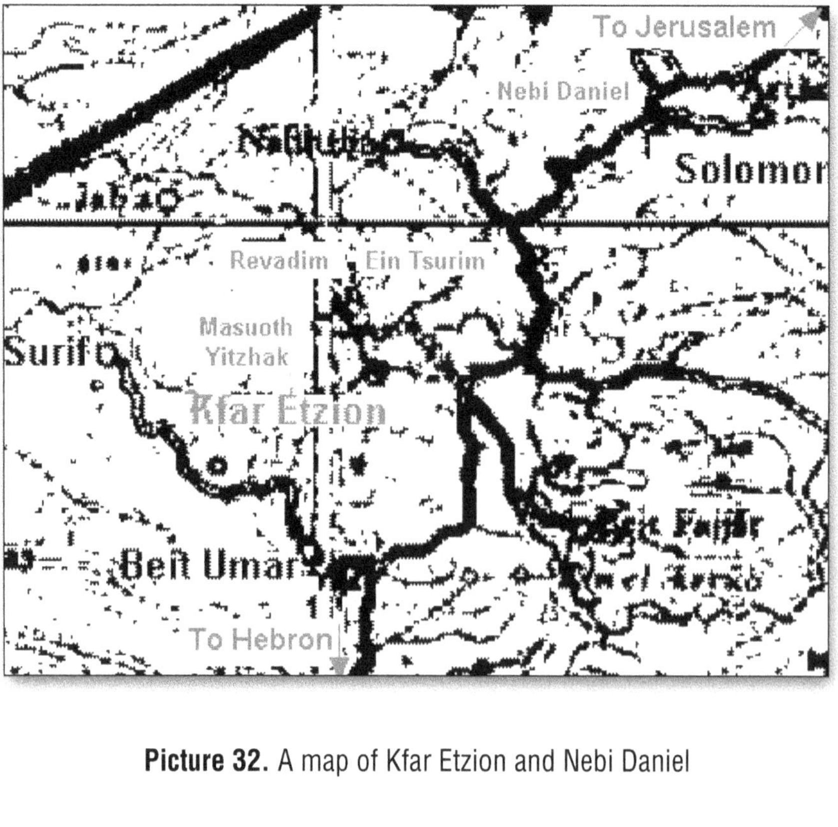

Picture 32. A map of Kfar Etzion and Nebi Daniel

I was listening to a radio (a rare device in those days) and realized that my comrades in the convoy were in a desperate situation and were requesting assistance. They demanded, "Send birds— this is urgent." It appeared to me that it would be possible to save the convoy by applying a smoke screen and tear gas. With this idea, I approached the district commander of the Haganah, located at the Jewish Agency building on King George Street, and offered my help. I was told that the Red Cross and the British Army would evacuate the besieged comrades and leave their guns to the attackers. Yehuda Venezia, a pioneer of the Palmach and an expert in mining and demolition, recalls:

> Amos Chorev left Jerusalem and came to Tel Aviv, via the Burma Road.[12] He entered the "Red House" on Yarkon Street in Tel Aviv, where Ben-Gurion had his headquarters. Chorev shouted: "My soldiers are facing serious danger. We have to help them by bombing with our aircraft." Haim Singer, who was the demolition commander of the Palmach, asked what had happened. Chorev replied: "Our convoy was delayed in Kfar Etzion. During that time, Arabs blocked the road leading to Jerusalem. The convoy left Kfar Etzion, reached Nebi Daniel, and was stuck there, as the road was blocked. At this moment, thousands of Arabs are attacking our soldiers, who have moved to an isolated building and are entrenched there."
>
> Immediately, I went to our hardware store, opened it (it was the Sabbath) and retrieved three-inch diameter pipes. I brought the pipes to the "Kirya" (formerly Sarona, a settlement founded by German Templers), filled

---

12 The Burma Road: the Israeli "Burma Road" was a makeshift bypass road between the general vicinity of Kibbutz Hulda and Jerusalem. It was built by Israeli forces headed by General Mickey Marcus during the 1948 siege of Jerusalem. The name was inspired by the Burma Road in China.

them with TNT, and attached a fifteen-second delay fuse to each pipe. This delay time was selected so that the "bombs" thrown from these places would explode when they hit the ground.

We prepared more than one hundred of these "bombs" and then rushed back to the "Red House," where many leaders had assembled for an emergency meeting with Ben-Gurion. Yitzhak Rabin entered, described the situation, and recommended that we rescue our besieged soldiers by bombing the attackers from the air. Moshe Sharett, one of the most important diplomats of the Jewish Agency, shouted: "Do not do this! It is against the conventions. We will negotiate with British officials and they will rescue them." Rabin asked me, "How many 'bombs' did you prepare?" I answered, "More than one hundred." Ben-Gurion then told Rabin, "You have twenty minutes to transfer the 'bombs' to Sde Dov.[13] Use Piper aircraft to bomb the Arab attackers." (16)

According to Uri Littauer, he was one of those who prepared the "bombs" by filling the pipes with TNT. This was one of the contributions of HEMED to that operation. Uzi Narkis[14] described the event in his book *Soldier of Jerusalem*:

On Friday March 26, 1948, I landed at Sde Dov after transferring the command of Kfar Etzion to my successor. On Saturday, I went to Palmach headquarters and looked for a new appointment. On the second floor, I saw Yitzhak Rabin and Yigal Allon[15] studying a map.

---

13 Sde Dov is an airport located in northern Tel Aviv, not far from the beach.

14 Uzi Narkis was an Israeli general and commander of the central region during the Six-Day War.

15 Yigal Allon was a commander of the Palmach and a general in the IDF.

Yigal [Allon] told me, "The convoy is stuck. Rush to Sde Dov, take an airplane, fly over the convoy, and report to me."

In the meantime, thousands of Arabs had gathered along the road to Jerusalem and started to block it. The armored car, which was the first in the convoy, crossed the first roadblock, but stopped at another one near Nebi Daniel, south of Bethlehem. Ten cars turned around and returned to Kfar Etzion. Forty-one cars were stuck and some two hundred soldiers were trapped. For more than thirty hours our soldiers exchanged fire with Arab attackers. I returned to Palmach headquarters and reported what I saw from the plane. Amos Chorev had the brilliant idea of bombing them from the air. We rushed to Yehuda Venezia's hardware store and took 25-millimeter diameter pipes. Amos cut the pipes into 10-centimeter-long pieces and filled them with explosives and primers. We packed these primitive "bombs" into baskets and climbed into a plane. The pilot was sitting behind me and in the front there were two open windows, through which "bombs" could be thrown.

We flew over the battle field and I threw the "bombs" on the crowd that was attacking our forces. Some of the "bombs" hit the ground but did not stop the attackers. When the basket was empty, I returned to Sde Dov. There, I found out that several other planes had repeated our bombing activities, also dropping ammunition and supplies. (17)

2. The Old City of Jerusalem

The Jewish Quarter of the Old City of Jerusalem was cut off from the western part of the city and the entrance through the Jaffa Gate was blocked. In May, approximately 1,700 people (among them elderly people and children) were living in the Jewish Quarter. One hundred and forty eight fighters (about 40% from the Irgun and the rest from the Haganah) and some fifty service personnel were recruited from among the residents of the quarter.

Avraham Halperin was appointed commander of the Jewish Quarter of Jerusalem by the Haganah. He won the trust of those around him. He enforced order and discipline in the Haganah units and organized the somewhat problematic civilian population. On March 3, 1948, he was expelled from the Old City by the British Police and followed by Motke Pinkas. Moshe Rosnak was the last commander of the Jewish Old City who surrendered to the Arab Legion.

The defenders had 300 bullets for each rifle, and 500 for each machine-gun. In addition, there were 374 hand-grenades, 126 assault grenades, and 200 kilograms of explosives. Obviously, this was not sufficient for the defense of the Old City.

Convoys, which entered through the Jaffa Gate, brought supplies to the residents of the Jewish Quarter of the Old City. As Arab onslaughts increased, convoys were instructed to drive through the Zion Gate, a less dangerous route, since it did not traverse Arab neighborhoods. After the British entered the Old City, they undertook to escort the convoys, but they prevented the transfer of arms and fighters to the Jewish Quarter. While it would have been possible to smuggle in young people in the guise of teachers or social workers, the Haganah chose not to exploit this tactic to smuggle in military equipment.

I was asked to try to smuggle ingredients for the preparation of Molotov cocktails into the Old City (see Picture 17). Molotov cocktails are crude incendiary weapons that consist of a glass bottle filled with a flammable liquid, usually gasoline. I was aware that gasoline and crepe (a rubber-like material used to make the fluid more viscous) were needed for the preparation of this weapon. They were poured into bottles, which were then

wrapped with a cloth containing sugar and an oxidant, usually potassium chlorate. A glass tube containing sulfuric acid
was attached to the cloth. When the tube was broken, the sulfuric acid was spilled over the cloth, heat was generated, and the
cloth ignited. Packing gasoline, sugar, and chlorate was relatively easy, as they could be seen as innocent substances. On the
other hand, sending sulfuric acid was difficult. It occurred to
me that batteries for cars or electricity contained sulfuric acid.
So I went to Mr. Battish, the drugstore owner, who kindly provided me with sulfuric acid (free of charge!). These "innocent"
materials were loaded onto a truck, passed the inspection of
British policemen, and were received by the defenders of the
Jewish Quarter. Eventually, this was the only anti-tank weapon
used against the armored cars of the Arab Legion that penetrated into the Old City.

As the supply of grenades dwindled, Emmanuel Meidav
began to produce them in the quarter. With the help of Leah
Woltz and a group of boys, he went from house to house col-
lecting empty tin cans, which were then filled with nails and
explosives. During the fighting in the Old City, the improvised
arms factory produced more than 2,500 grenades, thanks to
which the defenders managed to hold out for a considerably
longer time than anticipated. Unfortunately, one of the grenades exploded in Emmanuel Meidav's hands. He was seriously
wounded and passed away on May 19, 1948. Meidav did not
have conventional explosives (such as TNT) to fill his hand grenades, and so he used the inferior cheddite, which was also used
in the New City of Jerusalem.

In Jerusalem, there was a shortage of detonators, the devices used to trigger explosive materials. It was decided to establish a plant in which these dangerous devices could be manufactured. Who could be in charge of such a dangerous mission?
The obvious choice was Emmanuel Goldschlag-Meron, who
was an expert in the production of explosives and did not hesi-

tate to accept this appointment. We found a small building in Romema, and Goldschlag-Meron started to produce detonators, or "dets" as we called them. Soon we realized that Goldschlag-Meron, who was deaf, could not hear when one of the detonators fell on the floor of his laboratory. There was a danger that he might step on one of them and cause an explosion. We solved this problem by training a dog, who we named Ten, to pull on Goldschlag-Meron's trousers if anything fell on the floor. By doing this we saved Goldschlag-Meron's life and the production of detonators proceeded smoothly. Whenever we needed "dets" for field experiments, we approached Emmanuel Goldschlag-Meron (see Picture 33 for an example).

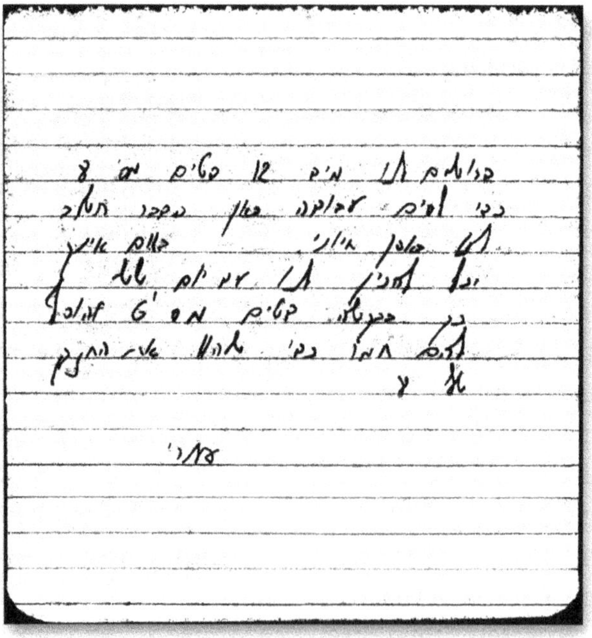

Picture 33. A request for "dets" from by Uri Littauer, commander of the Chemical Unit. Translated from the Hebrew, the text reads: "We need 12 No. 8 'dets' to finish an experiment. We need them immediately. If you cannot prepare them by Friday, please use No. 6 and add more explosives so that they resemble No. 8. Signed, Uri.

Picture 34. A simple land-mine produced by us.

After preparing detonators and after completing the production of the cheddite, we began to produce land mines (Picture 34). We found a workshop near the Machane Yehuda market in Jerusalem, where the owner Mr. Tchursh had a furnace for melting metals. The heat of the furnace was relatively low, so it could melt only aluminum, zinc, or tin, but iron could not be cast. We prepared wooden frames into which aluminum-zinc alloys were cast. These molds were then filled with explosives, mainly cheddite. The primitive mines were then given to various units that fortified the borders of Jerusalem.

We started our activities in the New City of Jerusalem, but most of our equipment and chemicals were left at the Mount Scopus campus of The Hebrew University. This campus was isolated, and only protected convoys could reach it. I joined one of these convoys and succeeded in bringing back bottles of sulfuric acid, which were later used for the production of Molotov cocktails. On April 13, 1948, a convoy attempted to reach Mount Scopus but was ambushed in the Arab neighborhood of Sheikh Jarach. Seventy-eight passengers of the convoy were killed and from that day on, there was almost no access to Mount Scopus, and no equipment could be transferred from Mount Scopus to members of HEMED in downtown Jerusalem.

E. Ben-Gurion and the Formation of HEMED

David Ben-Gurion began to study Turkish law in Istanbul at the beginning of the twentieth century, but he never completed his studies. He was an autodidact, appreciated science, and respected scientists. It is likely that his daughter Renana was influenced by him. She became a scientist, worked at the Israel Institute for Biological Research in Ness Ziona, and was also active in HEMED in Jerusalem in 1948.

In April 1987, the Israel Academy of Science and Humanities celebrated the one-hundredth anniversary of the birth of Ben-Gurion. In the opening lecture, Prof. Joshua Jortner, president of the academy, cited a presentation by Ben-Gurion at the seventh meeting of the first Knesset:

> In our generation, we have witnessed the greatest revolution in human history. We see that human beings can control the power of nature. We can control the atom and space and uncover the mystery of the universe. We cannot compare our nation to others in terms of numbers, wealth, and power, but our intellectual and human resources are not less than those of other nations. This is our inheritance, which is based on the history of the Jewish people, saturated with suffering and devotion. We can use theoretical and applied science to absorb new immigrants, improve education, strengthen our security, and develop our economy. In this respect we are not less productive than other developed nations. This is our mission and we will do our best to achieve our goals (18, translated from the Hebrew).

At the first meeting of the Israel Academy of Science and Humanities, on February 23, 1960, Ben-Gurion said:

> We were always a small nation with a small country and we were not blessed by nature, but there is no doubt

that we were blessed by mental superiority. Our nation, which could create books like the Bible, can in our days also contribute much to the progress of science (19, translated from the Hebrew).

Ben-Gurion was very disturbed by the fact that many Jewish scientists and other intellectuals did not emphasize their Jewish origin. He believed that this situation would change in the State of Israel and that local scientists, authors, and scholars would be proud of their Jewish legacy. Indeed, this actually happened and Israelis have received Nobel Prizes in literature (Agnon) and science (Hershko, Ciechanover, Aumann, and Yonath).

At the same meeting of the Israel Academy of Science and Humanities, Ephraim Katzir stated:

Ben-Gurion respected basic and applied science, mainly, when he prepared himself for the establishment of a Jewish State. He became interested in recent developments in science and tried to widen his outlook through conversations with leading scientists in Israel and to learn about their achievements (20, translated from the Hebrew).

In light of his interest in science, it is not surprising that Ben-Gurion met frequently with Aharon and Ephraim Katchalsky and discussed chemistry and biology problems with them. The secrets of the atom were revealed to him by E.D. Bergmann. At this meeting, Ephraim Katzir cited a paragraph from Ben-Gurion's book:

Through science, men can control nature. This is based on their ability to reveal the secrets of nature and to subdue them to his service. We live in a generation in which the secrets of the atom were disclosed and new sources of energy were discovered. In our generation, new dimensions of space were revealed and new aspects in the research of chemistry and bacteriology improved the production of crops and changed the basic principles of agriculture. Improved technologies increased the yield of industry and now we operate in the following three dimensions: earth, air, and below the sea. Until now, we have scattered our intellectual treasures among foreign nations and helped different countries to promote science in the fields of chemistry, mathematics, biology, and technology. It is very likely that in their homeland, Israeli scientists will promote science for the benefit of the world and for the reputation of their nation (21, translated from the Hebrew).

General Yohanan Ratner was born in 1891 in Russia and served as an officer in the Red Army during World War I. Thereafter, he studied architecture in Germany and immigrated to Palestine, where he became commander in chief of the Haganah and took an active part in the formation of the Palmach. On page 338 of his book (22) and translated from the Hebrew, he describes Ben-Gurion as having "a mystical belief in science" and being "convinced that science [could] solve problems. He was one of the few leaders who were personally involved in solving problems. Once he told me, 'Listen, we have to recruit all of our forces, including scientists, who will contribute much to our potential.'"

F. The Israel Military Industries (Taas)

From the early 1930s, members of the Haganah started to produce weapons and ammunition. During World War II, scientists from The Hebrew University in Jerusalem supplied the allied forces with crystals for optical instruments, which were urgently needed. In addition, parasitologists from The Hebrew University served as officers in the British armed forces and helped them to control tropical diseases. The Haganah used the experience of these scientists for training and weapons production.

In October 1947, Ben-Gurion, who was at the time head of the Jewish Agency, planned the formation of a committee to begin scientific military research (23). Yohanan Ratner was appointed director, E.D. Bergmann, G. Racah, and H. Heimann were members, and Aharon Katchalsky was secretary. The committee was responsible for controlling the budget and planning scientific activities. Ben-Gurion respected Aharon Katchalsky as a scientist and as a human being. Therefore, it is not surprising that Katchalsky succeeded in securing funds from Ben-Gurion. Ratner convinced Yitzhak Sadeh, commander of the Palmach, to contribute 150 Sterling pounds (23). Ben-Gurion appreciated the importance of the committee, and at the end of 1947, he donated another 200 pounds. He promised to allocate 10,000 pounds annually. Aharon Katchalsky was surprised and did not know what to do with this considerable sum.

Ben-Gurion, with his vision, was very instrumental in stimulating scientists to work in the fields of military chemistry and physics. He attempted to supply them with means and resources to the best of his ability. Ben-Gurion was one of the few prime ministers who believed that we had the ability to produce new weapons and improve existing ones. Yitzhak Rabin, who also served as prime minister, was not convinced that our scientists could contribute much to our security. He preferred to buy sophisticated weapons from foreign sources and not to "waste" money by paying our scientists.

In July 1943, Aharon Katchalsky, the philosopher Yeshayahu Leibowitz, and the public relations expert Moshe Brill published a book titled *Scientific Discoveries and Warfare* (24) (in Hebrew). It appears that Ben-Gurion studied this book and was influenced by its content. Ben-Gurion was also influenced by the British tradition. During World War II, a scientific body was created in the United Kingdom and named the "Back Room." It was divided into three sections: A-atomic, B-biological, and C-chemical. Ben-Gurion adopted this model and when HEMED was created, three similar sections were established for research and defense.

In 1947, Nigel Balchin published his book *The Small Back Room* (25), in which he described the activities of British scientists. The scientific unit was headed by Prof. Meyer, who had close links with several high officials in the government. The scientists tried to use their previous experience to solve military problems. Thus, they evaluated their results statistically and did not care if the rockets fell near the shooters and not near the target, provided that the results were statistically satisfactory. Military personnel, however, were not interested in statistics. They wanted to hit their targets. Therefore, the Army did not communicate with the scientists, who were not asked to solve military problems. (On the other hand, it should be noted that during World War II, important discoveries were made in the United Kingdom. These included the production of penicillin, which saved many lives, and radar.)

When we became active in HEMED, we studied the book and drew the following three conclusions: 1) Do not develop a new weapon if the Army is not interested in it; 2) An operations unit is needed, so that scientists can apply their findings to the battlefield; and 3) Whenever the Army has a problem or request, scientists should respond immediately.

G. How Did the System Function?

Nathan Arad, the son of Yitzhak Vilenchuk, provided me with a document that read as follows:

Taas was founded in the 1920s in response to the riots and attacks on Jewish settlements in 1921. The Haganah needed weapons and ammunition to defend the population. Indeed, hand grenades were manufactured in primitive workshops, hidden from the British government (26, translated from the Hebrew).

Dr. Asher Shamgar, who was called "the doctor," was certainly one of the founders of the military industry in Palestine. In Rehovot, he opened a small laboratory in an orange juice factory (Jafora), where he produced cordite (a family of smokeless propellants developed and produced in the United Kingdom from 1889 to replace gunpowder as a military propellant). See Picture 35.

Picture 35. Cordite

In 1940, Shamgar moved from Rehovot to Kfar Vitkin and manufactured the so-called "Polish" hand grenade, which exploded when its handle was lifted. The explosive known as "ten" (penta-erythritol-tetranitrate) was also manufactured at the same plant (27).

The riots that took place from 1936 to 1939 promoted an increase in weapons production. As a result, four new "institutes" were opened in Tel Aviv, Haifa, Rehovot and Jerusalem, where two- and three-inch mortars and their shells were manufactured. During World War II, weapons could not be smuggled from Europe. Therefore, Taas manufactured hundreds of mortars and thousands of shells, and attempts were made to produce Sten submachine guns (26).

After World War II, from 1945 to 1947, additional institutes were opened under the leadership of Joseph Avidar. Avidar (born Yosef Rochel, 1906–1995) was one of the founders of the Haganah and one of its senior commanders. He founded new facilities, including the secret Ayalon Institute, for weapons production. A delegation headed by Yaakov Dori, who was the Haganah chief of staff, was sent to the United States in 1946–1947 to purchase arms. In the United States, Dori and Chaim Slavin (the head of Taas) purchased tools that were used for the production of bullets and explosives.

At the end of 1947, it was clear that a Jewish State would be established and the neighboring Arab countries would attack us. Ben-Gurion realized that our military arsenal was not sufficient and decided to increase weapons production. In December 1947, he and Levi Eshkol (founder of the Histadrut—the General Federation of Laborers—and the third prime minister of the State of Israel) appointed the engineer Yitzhak Vilenchuk to head an Emergency Military Industries Committee. The members of the committee were Chaim Slavin, head of Taas, and HEMED representatives Prof. Yohanan Ratner and Shlomo Gur. The "doctor," Raanan Weitz, and Shlomo Bogard represented the chemical industries. The Special Operation Unit was headed by Simcha Blass. All these units and divisions functioned separately in different parts of the country, concealed from the eye of the British Police. For important meetings, Levi Eshkol and Yaakov Dori were also invited.

Usually the Emergency Military Industries Committee operated as follows: The headquarters of the Haganah was interested in obtaining bombs, mortars, explosives, mines, and/or shells. HEMED received the order and planned the mechanical or chemical parts of the weapon. Thereafter, Yitzhak Vilenchuk ordered the different mechanical parts from various private workshops. The Chemical Unit dealt with the production of explosives and smoke screens. Simcha Blass, with his Special Operation Unit, attempted to copy foreign weapons, such as flame throwers and PIAT (Projector Infantry Anti-Tank), an anti-tank weapon (Picture 36). It was very difficult to coordinate actions between the different bodies, which were in charge of the production of various parts. Sometimes errors prevented the assembly of the parts, and the production of the weapon was delayed.

In the middle of November 1947, it was clear that Arab countries would start a war. The Haganah started to train new field brigades and Ben-Gurion invited several military experts for consultations. They included Israel Galili, national commander of the Haganah; Yaakov Dori, the chief of staff of the Haganah; Levi Eshkol; and Shaul Avigur, who was a founder of the Israeli intelligence community. In some meetings, Prof. Yohanan Ratner, who organized the scientific unit of the Haganah, and Chaim Slavin of Taas also participated (27).

Picture 36. Projector Infantry Anti-Tank (PIAT) Weapon

At first, the Haganah industry copied existing weapons. Only later trained manpower and improved equipment permitted the production of newly designed arms. The personal relationships between Taas and HEMED were far from ideal, and friction between Chaim Slavin (from Taas) and Jenka Ratner (from HEMED) prevented the production of the PIAT.

The development of the research and development of Israeli armaments can be summarized as follows:

1. March 1938–1948: the Scientific Department of the Haganah

2. 1948–1952: the Scientific Corps of the Israeli Army (HEMED)

3. 1952–1958: the Research and Development Division of the Ministry of Defense

4. 1958–2001: the Armament Development Authority, Advanced Defense Systems (Rafael), attached to the Ministry of Defense

5. 2001–present: Rafael Ltd., a government-controlled company. (28)

CHAPTER 5:

THE FORMATION OF THE SCIENCE CORPS

A. Functions of the Corps

The Science Corps was officially created on March 17, 1948, when the deputy chief commander of the Army, Major General Zvi Ayalon, issued the following order:

1. It has been decided to form a Scientific Research Department under the command of the Chief of Staff.

2. The Scientific Unit will be a part of the Scientific Research Department.

3. Following are the tasks of the Unit:

    a. To carry out military-oriented research

    b. To carry out field tests based on the military-oriented research

    c. To instruct military units on the use of the developed weapons

    d. To assist in the development of new military industries and improve contacts with existing plants

---

4. Number 548 was assigned to the Scientific Unit and details will be attached.

5. The activities of the Unit will begin on the date of this document.

6. Requests for equipment, armaments, and means of transportation should be submitted to the Chief of Staff before April 1, 1948.

7. Means of communication and medical supplies will be provided by the Chief of Staff before April 1, 1948.

8. The name HEMED has been officially approved for Scientific Unit No. 548.

9. Abraham Berman was appointed deputy commander of the Scientific Unit.

10. The Scientific Unit will have an independent budget.

Signed, Boaz (acronym used by Ayalon in the underground of Haganah)

In the name of the Chief of Staff [29, translated from the Hebrew]

B. HEMED Staff and Base Commanders in Jerusalem and Haifa

On April 2, 1948, two weeks after the publication of the order issued by the chief of staff, Abraham Berman issued the following document (courtesy of Uriel Littauer):

To HEMED Staff Members and Base Commanders in Jerusalem and Haifa:

Uriel Littauer has been appointed commander of the Chemical Unit.

Heini Fry has been appointed temporary commander of the physicists and engineers.

Alon Feldman[-Radler-Talmi] has been appointed officer of administration.

Aharon Strikovsky has been appointed officer of operations.

Haim Murro has been appointed officer of industry.

Tuvia Berlin has been appointed commander of the Jerusalem base.

Moshe Ish-Shalom has been appointed commander of the Haifa base.

A special order will be issued for the appointment of commanders of platoons, services, and the commanding units of the different bases. [translated from the Hebrew]

Abraham Berman planned to organize HEMED as a military unit, to divide it into companies and platoons, but this plan never came to fruition.

CHAPTER 6:

INSTITUTES IN TEL AVIV

A. The "Studio"

At the end of 1947, the "Studio" was the center of pre-HEMED activities in Tel Aviv. Shlomo Gur and Jenka Ratner met in the office of architect Yaakov Rechter at 8 Engel Street in Tel Aviv. They decided to recruit several engineers to develop new armaments. Later, the activity moved to the "Studio" in Frug Street. There, Aharonchik Donagi and Haim Murro joined Rechter and Moshe Zarchi and were instructed to design the production of land mines and flame throwers. Amos De Shalit and Gideon Yekutieli, physicists from Jerusalem, also joined the group in the "Studio" (30). A. Eisenfeld states in his dissertation *The Roots of the Science Corps (HEMED) in the Haganah*:

When Jenka Ratner returned from the United Kingdom to Tel Aviv, he was given a room in the [two-room] apartment of Shlomo Gur [...] He was given a desk which was used by Gili, Shlomo's daughter. When Jenka's work increased, he had to move to a new house in Frug Street. An asbestos roof was added on the balcony and after it was closed, the balcony became the first office of the Scientific Department and later of HEMED. This was the beginning of the famous "Studio" (31, translated from the Hebrew).

When HEMED Base No. 1 was established on the "Hill," architects Zarchi and Rechter moved their offices to this new location in the newly formed base. A close collaboration between architects, chemists, and physicists commenced. Among other projects, they designed and developed the M-2 and M-3 cannons.

B. *Machon Hetekanim* (Israel Standards Institute) in Tel Aviv

The Israel Standards Institute for quality control was located at 200 Dizengoff Street in Tel Aviv. It was equipped with modern analytical instruments, and it was here that scientists conducted tests for the Haganah, even before the foundation of the first HEMED base (Base No.1 on the "Hill"). Analytical chemists from this institute helped to analyze products obtained from the chemists of HEMED. HEMED seminars and workshops were also held there.

Nathan Shtrikman (Sharon) was one of the HEMED scientists who began research at the institute (32). Shtrikman (Picture 37) was born in Tel Aviv on November 4, 1925, and studied at Balfour High School. In 1941, he joined the Haganah, like many of his classmates. During his training in the Gadna,[16] he marched from Tel Hai to Hanita in the Galilee. There he saw members of the Palmach armed with illegal rifles. Based on this encounter, he decided to join the Palmach after graduating from high school. Yitzhak Pundak, who was his company commander in the Gadna, was one of the commanders of the

---

16 Gadna is an Israeli military program to prepare youth for their military service. At the time, it prepared them for service in the Haganah.

Givati Brigade in the War of Independence. Other members of his group were Aharon Davidi, who became the commander of the Israeli paratroopers, and Aharonchik Donagi. Bracha Fuld also belonged to this group. Fuld was a member of the Palmach who took part in the planned landing of the refugee ship that was to come ashore on the Tel Aviv beachfront. She was killed by British soldiers.

At the beginning of 1943, members of the Palmach came to Shtrikman's class to persuade him and his classmates to join this unit of the Haganah after their graduation. Shtrikman was convinced and joined the Palmach, which at that time had around seven hundred volunteers. He joined Company D and worked in the Ramat Hakovesh orange plantation, kitchen, and bakery fourteen days each month. During the rest of the time, he underwent training. The arrangement for Palmach members

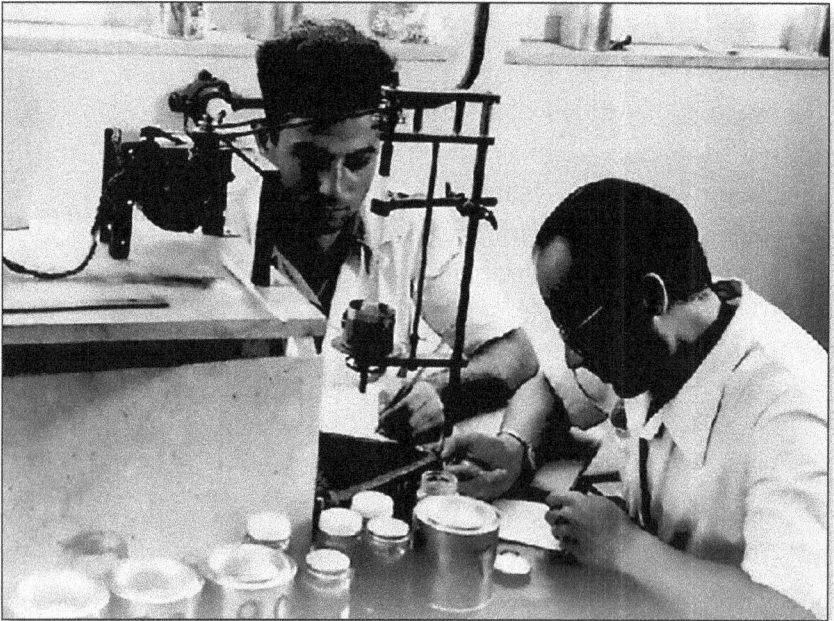

Picture 37. Nathan Sharon and Leon Bloch measuring the viscosity of napalm at the Israel Standards Institute

was that they stayed in kibbutzim, where they were supplied with food and accommodations, and were required to work two weeks each month to cover expenses.

In October 1943, Shtrikman and his company completed their training and a graduation ceremony was planned. To make this ceremony more impressive, rifles had to be brought by platoon commanders from their hiding places. They had to smuggle the arms from another kibbutz, traveling by bus. Unfortunately, the bus was stopped and searched by British policemen, who found the guns and arrested the platoon commanders. Soon thereafter, British soldiers surrounded the kibbutz where Company D was camped and arrested Shtrikman along with thirty-five of his comrades.

They were beaten and transferred to a prison in Nablus. After several weeks, they were released from the prison, but Company D was transferred to another kibbutz to avoid the surveillance of the British Police. Shtrikman served in the Palmach for two years, unlike his comrades, who served for only one. He was put in charge of storing and concealing illegal weapons, a very difficult and demanding task. In the autumn of 1945, Shtrikman commenced his studies at The Hebrew University of Jerusalem. In 1946, he was asked to join a secret team that developed illegal arms and explosives. The secret activities were carried out at night in the laboratories of The Hebrew University, which were empty during the late hours. He was instructed to develop napalm (naphthenic and palmitic acids), which served as fuel for flame throwers (32).

At the end of 1947, when the War of Independence began, Shtrikman was recruited by the Palmach as a member of the "reserve" unit. He escorted convoys, hiding his illegal guns (mainly assisted by girls who concealed pistols or hand grenades in their clothing). In mid-December 1947, he was asked by Zvi Zamir, the commander of Battalion 6 of the Palmach, to bring sulfuric acid from Aharon Katchalsky's laboratory on Mount Scopus in

Jerusalem. This acid was needed by Battalion 6 for the preparation of Molotov cocktails. When Shtrikman arrived on Mount Scopus he found some of his colleagues in Aharon Katchalsky's laboratory. They included Heini Eisenberg, Uri Littauer, and Yehuda Mazur, whom he knew as students of chemistry. When Aharon Katchalsky saw him, he greeted him and said, "Welcome! We have been looking for you. We plan to form a scientific unit and you should join it." Actually, this was the first group from which HEMED emerged.

Shtrikman planned to marry Rachel in Tel Aviv on January 13, 1948. It was very difficult to travel from Jerusalem to Tel Aviv, but Shtrikman made it. In Tel Aviv, he met with Shlomo Gur, who asked him to continue his research on napalm at the Israel Standards Institute.

After the end of the War of Independence, Shtrikman changed his family name to Sharon and started to work on his PhD dissertation at the faculty of agriculture in Rehovot. Thereafter, he joined the Weizmann Institute in Rehovot, was promoted to the rank of professor, and gained a worldwide reputation based on his research on lectins and carbohydrates. He was elected a member of the Israel Academy of Science and Humanities, awarded the Israel Prize, and came to be regarded as one of the leading scientists in Israel. He passed away on June 17, 2011.

At the Israel Standards Institute, Sharon continued his research on napalm together with Leon Bloch, a senior scientist at the institute. They studied the viscosity of the napalm fluid using a cuvette viscositometer (Picture 37). They were aided by Prof. Markus Reiner, a well-known rheologist from the Technion in Haifa. Gideon Blauer moved from Jerusalem and joined the group, as did Yeshayahu Gallili (Picture 38).

Yeshayahu (Shaya) Gallili was born in Ukraine on November 13, 1925. His mother, Devora, was a descendent of the family of the famous Rabbi of Lubavitch and grew up in a small village as a farmer. After studying agronomy, she immigrated to Palestine and taught agronomy at the Ben Shemen Youth Village.

Picture 38. Captain Yeshayahu Gallili

Several years later, she moved to Tel Aviv. Her son studied at the A.D. Gordon Beit Chinuch School, where Yitzhak Rabin also studied. During his studies he became a member of Ha-shomer Hatzair, a progressive Zionist youth movement.[17]

In 1944, Shaya Galili began his studies at The Hebrew University of Jerusalem and planned to specialize in physical chemistry. His studies were interrupted at the end of 1947, when the struggle for independence started. He was stationed at the university campus on Mount Scopus in April 1948 and saw that the convoy to Mount Scopus was trapped at Sheikh Jarach and seventy-eight of the passengers were killed. While looking at the

---

17 Hashomer Hatzair is a progressive Zionist youth movement and specializes in youth-led experiential Jewish education based on the values of equity.

attacked convoy, he noticed that one of the passengers escaped from a burning armored car and was crawling in the direction of Mount Scopus. It was extremely dangerous to rescue him, as snipers were shooting at him constantly. Despite the danger, Gallili crawled in his direction and dragged him to safety, even after being hit in the leg by a bullet. With his courageous act, he saved the life of the escaping soldier. Later, one of the soldiers was wounded near the fence of Mount Scopus. Again, a volunteer was needed to rescue him. Gallili, even after having been wounded, did not hesitate to save him. He approached the wounded soldier and then was hit by a bullet in the chest.

After recovering from his wounds, he was transferred from Jerusalem to Tel Aviv and joined Nathan Sharon's napalm research group. In Ness Ziona, another HEMED base was established. In 1954, a group of physical chemists formed a team that specialized in the research of aerosols (a suspension of fine solid particles or liquid droplets in a gas) and the development of masks for protection against toxic materials. Shaya Gallili, Shlomo Dvir, and Gedalia Volenitz were members of this team. Aharon Katchalsky, who returned to his scientific activities at the Weizmann Institute, invited Gallili to work for his PhD under his guidance.

Galili accepted this invitation and in 1956 he received his doctorate. Thereafter, he moved to the United States with his wife Ruth for his post-doctoral training. He worked at Columbia University in New York from 1956 to 1957 and at the University of Illinois from 1957 to 1958. In 1958, he returned to his laboratory in Ness Ziona and continued his previous research on aerosols. He became a worldwide expert on aerosols and was invited to work at Johns Hopkins University in Baltimore and universities in Germany and Taiwan. During his research in Ness Ziona, he constructed furnaces made of asbestos, which affected his health. In 1969, he was appointed professor at the Department of Atmosphere Sciences at The Hebrew University of Jerusalem (33), when Zvi Pelach tested the velocity of explosion waves, an accident occurred and he was injured. Shaya Gallili heard the explosion, removed him from the site, and transferred him to a hospital. "I will never forget this. I always respected Shaya for his gallant behavior," said Zvi Pelach (34).

Gallili complained of breathing difficulties and it soon became clear that he was suffering from lung cancer, which was the result of his work with asbestos in Ness Ziona. All attempts to save his life failed and he passed away in 1988. The Ministry of Defense accepted responsibility for his disease and he was recognized as a victim of his military service (33). May his memory be blessed.

Shaya Gallili was not the only one who was a victim of accidents. At that time, there were no strict safety regulations and many scientists and technicians were injured. In some cases, accidents resulted in death. Another victim of the negligence of safety was Zvi Appenschlag, who died as the result of an explosion. Kertesz was also killed in an explosion. According to Ephraim Katzir (35), Kertesz was asked by E.D. Bergmann to prepare a propellant[18] from guanidine perchlorate. When Kertesz attempted to prepare a pellet under high pressure, an explosion occurred, resulting in his death. In other HEMED units, there were more victims. A soldier named Pine who served in HEMED Company C was attacked by Bedouins. He was killed and his weapon was stolen (36). Accidents also occurred in HEMED Company B.

C. Agan Chemicals

Agan Chemicals was a cooperative organization for the production of chemicals and was the first chemical industry in the Middle East. It was founded in 1945 by Zvi Tzur, Michael

---

18 A propellant is a chemical used in the production of energy and pressurized gas to create movement of a fluid or to generate propulsion.

Pikarsky, and David Wofsi, all chemistry graduates of The Hebrew University of Jerusalem. Joel Avigan also joined the company at a later stage. At the beginning, the company's laboratory was located in Jerusalem, but later it moved to Motza, a suburb. According to Michael Pikarsky (37), joint activity with the Scientific Department of the Haganah was initiated in 1946. A special building was constructed for the production of chemicals for the Haganah and two chemists, Ruth Kort and Leah (the future wife of Michael Pikarsky), joined the group. The first product was the tear gas chloroacetophenone (or bromoacetophenone, according to Zvi Tzur).

At the beginning of the War of Independence, soldiers from Iraq conquered part of Motza and destroyed Agan's facilities. They broke the vessel containing the tear gas and had to escape because of the vapors. The lives of the chemists working at Agan were saved by Yigal Arnon, who was a guard at a children's home near the Agan facilities. As a result of that attack, the activities of Agan at Motza were stopped. The members of the company joined HEMED and moved to Base No.1 in Tel Haim.

Zvi Tzur, who was born in 1919, immigrated to Palestine in 1936 and enrolled at The Hebrew University (38). He was not accepted to the Department of Chemistry and therefore studied physics and mathematics for two years. He joined Agan after completing his studies and was responsible for the production of tear gas. In 1947, Agan produced several hundred kilograms of tear gas. Tzur also moved to HEMED Base No. 1 and together with Zelina Shatil produced several chemicals of military importance. After the War of Independence, Agan moved to Jaffa. Zvi Tzur was also instrumental in the creation of Makhteshim Agan, an agrochemical manufacturer and distributor of crop protection products in the Negev.

CHAPTER 7:

HEMED BASE NO. 1 IN TEL HAIM

A. Our Activities

At the beginning of April 1948, it was decided to create central bases for the activities of HEMED. This decision replaced previous plans to scatter scientists in various settlements to help in the production of explosives and assist in protecting them from enemy attacks. The increase in the number of recruits to HEMED was one reason for this decision. It had been proposed that the central base of HEMED should be close to Tel Aviv. There were a number of reasons for these plans. As mentioned above, according to the order of the chief of staff (March 17, 1948) HEMED was supposed to fulfill the following tasks: 1) carry out military-oriented research; 2) carry out field tests; 3) train military units to use weapons developed by its units; and 4) help to develop military industries. It soon became evident that the area near Tel Aviv was most suitable for these purposes. Near Tel Aviv, field tests could be carried out and training could take place in the adjacent camps (Sarona and Sarafend). Military industries already existed near Tel Aviv, for example at the Ayalon Institute near Rehovot. Bullets for Sten submachine guns had been manufactured there since 1946. It was conceivable that new weapons could also be produced at the same site.

On April 17, 1948, I was ordered to join a convoy leaving Jerusalem for Tel Aviv. This was one of the last convoys leaving for Tel Aviv, as the road was blocked at Bab el-Wad by Palestinian Arabs. I rushed home, packed my belongings, not forgetting my book on organic chemistry by Fieser and Fieser. I reached the convoy and was placed in one of the armored trucks. We passed Bab el-Wad, but after several kilometers we were attacked near the Arab village of Dir Ajub. Bullets hit our armored truck, but they did not cause any damage. On the other hand, unarmored trucks were heavily damaged.

Late in the evening, we arrived in Tel Aviv and were transferred to Tel Haim, near Ramat Gan. The place was deserted, but we found a building that we named the "Yellow House," which had previously belonged to the Wagner family, members of the German Templers. During World War II, German subjects who belonged to the Templers had been evacuated by the British to Australia. Therefore, some of the buildings were empty.

In the following days, we built some tents for our accommodation and started to construct a base that was later named HEMED Base No. 1 or the "Hill" (*Givah* in Hebrew). When we arrived there, we found trenches and Arabs who were still shooting from the village of Salama, which was not far away. There were also some empty houses, which belonged to Jewish families who had moved to other places because of the war. Salama was conquered only at the end of April 1948.

We constructed our tents between the trees of an orange orchard. My tent mates were: Shimon Gatt, Shmaya Ben-Moshe (an engineer who had graduated from the Technion and who later lost his life in a car accident), and Mordechai Rubin, an organic chemist who came to us from Boston. He was eventually appointed professor of chemistry at the Technion. We lived in our tent for more than one year and kept our belongings in a kitbag under our beds. We had to dig channels around our tents to prevent rain water from entering. Often we were awakened at night by frogs jumping on us. Picture 39 shows some of the Base No. 1 buildings sometime after its creation.

On March 18, 1948, Ben-Gurion wrote in his diary:

> I met with Shlomo Gur, Alon Feldman[-Radler-Talmi], and Abraham Berman from the Scientific Company. Currently, there are (on the base) 20 people, but their number will increase to 100. In Jerusalem and Haifa there will also be an additional 50 people. The base will be close to Givat Rambam, and for the time being they will be accommodated in tents (39, translated from the Hebrew).

Picture 39. HEMED Base No.1. The large building on the left was called the "Brown House."

One day later, on March 19, 1948, the chief of staff issued the following order:

Fortification of HEMED camp in Givat Rambam: You have to supply the building materials, but the constructions should be started by them. (40)

There is no evidence that the building materials were supplied by the Army. When the recruited guards came to the base in the middle of April, they could not detect a fence or a gate. Soon thereafter a number of huts were constructed, one serving as headquarters, another as a clinic. Josephine came from Romania, where she studied medicine and now served as a first aid nurse. We did not have a kitchen on the base and food was supplied by kitchens in Sarona. According to Uri Littauer, the headquarters of Base No. 1 included the following personnel (41):

Ephraim Katchalsky was appointed commander of HEMED. He was a well-known scientist and was respected by Ben-Gurion. During the British Mandate, he completed the officers' course of the Haganah and was commander of one of the Haganah companies in Jerusalem. In April 1948, he returned to Jerusalem after completing his research at Yale University in the United States. He was appointed commander of HEMED because of his military background and his good relationship with Ben-Gurion.

Abraham Berman was appointed deputy commander of HEMED, but served in this capacity only briefly.

Uriel Littauer was appointed commander of the Chemical Unit.

Ernst Fischer was appointed chief of military research.

Aharon Strikovsky was appointed commander of operation units.

Haim Murro was a member of the HEMED command and was responsible for contact with Taas to facilitate the production of the weapons developed by HEMED scientists. He was assisted by Aharon Donagi and Avraham Levy.

Alon Feldman-[Radler-Talmi] was appointed officer of administration, but he served in this capacity for only a short time and was replaced by Zvi Racheli, who was his adjutant.

Yitzhak Yashar was appointed as head of security.

Asher Asher was head of administration. He remained head of administration of HEMED from 1947 until 1950. At the end of 1947, Abraham Berman approached him and asked whether he would be willing to join the Scientific Department and organize it as a military unit. Asher was a member of the Palmach and thus had a military background. He had also a graduate of the School of Law and Economics in Tel Aviv and had an academic education. From his activities in the family business, he had gained experience in administration. His previous commander in the Palmach, Yitzhak Rabin, had agreed to transfer him from the Palmach to the Scientific Department (42). At the beginning of his work in the department, he met with Aharon Katchalsky and Alon Feldman-[Radler-Talmi] and it was decided to establish a base in Tel Haim. Subsequently, it was decided to create HEMED Company B.

This newly-formed unit was located in Jaffa in a building called Romano House. When more space was needed, the unit moved to several empty buildings in a suburb of Jaffa called Abu Kabir and HEMED Company B established its laboratories in this new location. In addition to his activities as an administrator, Asher Asher also took an active part in combat activities. He fought against Palestinian and Jordanian units near Beit Nabala, a Palestinian Arab village in the district of Ramla. There he used an M-2 canon produced by HEMED, equipped with hollow-charged shells (42).

After various weapons had been developed, it was decided to invite Yaakov Dori, chief of staff; Yigael Yadin, chief of operations of the Army; and General David Shaltiel, Jerusalem district commander for demonstrations. The firing of the M-2 canon was a great success and it was decided to continue its research and development. Attempts to fire from a recoilless gun were not successful.

The "Yellow House" in Tel Haim was converted into a club and in April 1948, furniture was brought, followed by a record player along with records of music in German for entertainment.

Ernst Fischer (Picture 40) was our director of military research. He divided us into research groups. Our group dealt with incendiary bombs and pyrotechnical weapons. Its members were Shimon Gatt (Grunwald), Shmaya Ben-Moshe, Mordechai Rubin, and me. Yehudit Birk produced flares and signals, while Nathan Sharon, Yeshayahu Gallili, and Arieh (Lola) Schweiger dealt with the fuel and ignition devices for flame throwers. Later, Yair Klivanski developed weapons containing tear gas.

Picture 40. Ernst Fischer, chief of military research

Fischer had a special personality. He was clever and modest. He allowed us the freedom to come up with crazy ideas, with the hope that one of them would prove to be of value. He was a PhD student in the Department of Physical Chemistry (headed by Prof. Farkash) at The Hebrew University. He inspired us greatly and stimulated our appetite for research in the years to come.

Fischer located us in an abandoned building (the "Grey House") in Tel Haim. We collected (stole) equipment and started our experiments. There was plenty of work and we needed assistants. Gideon Peleg (Pavlovic) was sent to the recruiting center to select some female soldiers who could help us in our work. We were very lucky and Nira Gur-Aryeh, Naomi Ben-Sira, Josepha Friedman, and Yaffa Kol joined us. They worked hard, sometimes exposed to explosives, and did their best to promote our research.

Uriel Littauer (Picture 41) was born in Tel Aviv in 1924. During his studies at Herzliya High School he joined the Haganah. After his graduation, he volunteered for the Palmach and became a member of Company F. He was sent to a platoon commanding course and took part in attacking Allenby Bridge on June 16, 1946. This was part of the action of the Haganah against the British administration in response to their interference with the immigration of Holocaust refugees.

Picture 41. Uriel Littauer, commander of the Chemical Unit

In 1944, Littauer began his chemistry studies at The Hebrew University. Based on his military background, Aharon Katchalsky appointed him commander of the Chemical Unit of HEMED. Subsequently, Littauer joined the Weizmann Institute and became one of the founders of the Department of Biochemistry. Later, he laid the foundation of the Department of Neurobiology, became its head, and served as a professor until his retirement. His contributions to Israeli science, mainly in the fields of biochemistry and neurobiology, were immense, and he was well recognized by the international scientific community. In 1965, he was elected president of the Israeli Biochemical Society, and, thanks to his international reputation, it became a member of the European Biochemical Societies (FEBS).

Because we were dealing with dangerous explosives, we received special boots with crepe rubber soles so that we could walk safely. We also received special overalls taken from the stores of the British Police forces at the Russian Compound in Jerusalem. They were part of the uniform of the Palestine Mobile Force (PMF).

In mid-May 1948, the Egyptian army invaded the southern part of Palestine (the Negev) and Egyptian planes attacked Tel Aviv. I realized that they were bombing the city without any resistance. I rushed to the armory, retrieved a Bren machine gun and ammunition, and decided to fire at the attacking planes, just to demonstrate resistance. On my way, I saw Adolf Levy, who had served in North Africa as a British soldier. I asked him to join me and we climbed up to the top of the "Yellow House." We propped our machine gun on the fence of the roof and tried to shoot. We soon realized that the angle was too low and that we could not hit the planes. I remembered the novel *For Whom the Bell Tolls* published by Ernest Hemingway in 1940 that described the civil war in Spain. According to the book, the gun was propped up on the shoulder of the hero's comrade, to gain the right angle for shooting. I adopted this scheme and placed the gun on Levy's shoulder and started shooting. I did not believe that I would be able to hit the attacking planes, but I could not sit idly by while Tel Aviv was being attacked.

Several days later, our camp was attacked by Egyptian planes, which dropped incendiary bombs. Fire broke out in the stores near our camp and we all rushed to the burning buildings, attempting to extinguish the fire. The following day, I went back to the site and found an unexploded 25-killogram incendiary bomb. I managed to disassemble it and study its composition (a dangerous task!).

In 1950, a lightweight automatic weapon was designed by Major Chaim Kara, head of the submachine gun section of the HEMED. Uzi Gal continued the development of the gun, which was named "Uzi" and manufactured by Taas (43). This was a valuable development, as the Uzi replaced the Sten gun (also manufactured by Taas), which had many drawbacks.

Based on the instructions of the chief of staff, one of the duties of HEMED scientists was to train new recruits. Zvi Pelach, who became an expert on explosives, trained new naval co-mando recruits (Palyam) at their base in Caesarea, on the Mediterranean coast about midway between Haifa and Tel Aviv. I was asked to train young officers at the officers' academy to use explosives for mining and demolition. I looked rather young and to make a more sincere impression, I decided to grow a mustache (Picture 42).

Picture 42.
The author as a young officer

B. Technical and Security Services

We concluded that trained technicians were essential for the progress of research and development. Skilled technicians in electronics and fine mechanics permitted the production of sophisticated arms by HEMED physicists and chemists.

1. Technicians

Technicians, who received their training in fine mechanics at the workshops of the Department of Physics at The Hebrew University and at the Brandeis Center, contributed much to the development of new weapons by HEMED scientists. They were also instrumental in designing and manufacturing the Uzi submachine gun.

Avraham Kedem was one of the technicians. He was born in Transylvania, immigrated to Palestine, and joined a kibbutz. After some time, he moved to Jerusalem and specialized in fine mechanics. He joined HEMED and worked in Jerusalem at the Schneller Base, where he designed the fuse for the Davidka mortar shells. Later, he left Jerusalem, moved to the Weizmann Institute in Rehovot, and designed fuses for the Israeli Navy (44).

2. Laboratory Assistants

Scientists, mainly chemists, conducted many experiments, and there was an urgent need to find technical assistants. Newly recruited women were asked to join HEMED and to help scientists in their work. None of them had any previous experience in laboratory work. Two of the newly recruited soldiers, Nira Gur-Aryeh and Naomi Ben-Sira, came from Kfar Vitkin, while Yaffa Kol came from the Beit Oved settlement near Rehovot (Picture 43). Mordechai Drory, who was a technician in the Department of Physical Chemistry at The Hebrew University, also joined HEMED. After completing his military service, he was sent by the Ministry of Foreign Affairs to France and later became ambassador of the State of Israel in France and Italy. The level of our technicians was certainly remarkable!

Picture 43. Laboratory technicians and guards. This picture was taken on June 27, 1948. Standing, from the right: Shoshana, Zippora, Bilhah, Joseph Hager (guard), Naomi Ben-Sira, Josepha Friedman, and Chana Aroch. Seated, from the right: Nira Gur-Aryeh, the author, Yaffa Kol. Front row: Meshulam (Shulik) Sapir and Bezalel Tidhar, guards.

3. Guards and Security Services

All the HEMED bases were regarded as top-secret units and confidential guards were needed to protect them. On April 14, 1948, Bezalel Tidhar and his classmate Meshulam (Shulik) Sapir reported to the recruiting center in Tel Aviv. Suddenly, they heard an announcement over the loudspeaker ordering them to report to headquarters. They obeyed the order and were met by an officer, who introduced himself as Yitzhak Yashar, a security officer of a top security unit. He asked them to join the unit and maintain its security. Both of them agreed and immediately received uniforms and were taken to HEMED Base No. 1 in Tel Haim. There they met with Abraham Berman, deputy commander of the base, who told them that they had just entered a top-security base, which was more secret than the nuclear center in Los Alamos, New Mexico. They were told that they would have to guard the base and prevent the entrance of spies interested in discovering our secrets. At that time, there was no fence around the base and Sapir, armed with a Sten gun, put up a sign that read "Stop!" at the entrance of the base (Picture 44).

Picture 44. Meshulam Sapir protecting the base

Base No. 1 was spread over a relatively large area, but no means of transportation for the guards were available. Therefore, Bezalel Tidhar decided to confiscate a donkey from the occupied Arab village of Salama and to use it as a "motorized vehicle" (Picture 45). Soon, Tidhar and Sapir realized that spies were not penetrating into the base and that their duties were boring and therefore requested to be transferred to another unit. It is remarkable that we had guards who were highly qualified and later played important roles as pilots in the Israeli Air Force. Sapir became a Wing Commander in the Air Force and later served as an Air Force attaché at the Israeli Embassy in Paris (45). Other guards are depicted in Picture 46.

Picture 45. Bezalel Tidhar riding on a donkey "motorized vehicle." In the background, some of the tents of the base are visible.

Picture 46. The guards of HEMED Base No. 1, April 1948. Standing from the right: Bezalel Tidhar (with a gun), Avraham Zeaman, Yitzhak Yashar (security officer), and Moshe Binnenholz. Kneeling from the right: Yehezkel Ben-Ari and Meshulam (Shulik) Sapir (courtesy of Tidhar).

4. Other Services

The number of female soldiers at HEMED Base No. 1 increased steadily. It was therefore decided to appoint a female officer to be in charge of them. Chana Grunwald, who later married Shimon Grunwald (Gatt), was appointed to command the women (Picture 47). She was accompanied by Sergeant Pirchia, who trained the newly recruited soldiers to use guns.

Picture 47. Chana Grunwald (Gatt), commander of the female soldiers (courtesy of Gabriella Fischer)

The commanders of the base succeeded in obtaining trucks and jeeps and Pardel was appointed to transportation officer. He also gave us driving lessons so that we could drive some of our jeeps.

A bunker for storing arms (rifles and machine guns) was also constructed along with another subterranean bunker for the storage of ammunition and explosives.

A motorcycle was used to connect our base with the head-quarters at the "Kirya" (formerly known as Sarona, a Templer colony). A new immigrant who did not speak Hebrew fell in love with the motorcycle and carried out many missions for our base. We did not know his name, but everybody called him *yingele*, which means "young boy" in Yiddish.

The chief of staff decided to appoint liaison officers to maintain contact and exchange information between the scientists of HEMED and the various army corps. Shaike Yarkoni served as the liaison offer between HEMED and the Air Force and was very helpful.

CHAPTER 8:

HEMED BASE NO. 2 IN JERUSALEM

As mentioned above, the The Hebrew University campus on Mount Scopus was cut off from the city of Jerusalem and only convoys could pass through the Mandelbaum Gate to provide food after inspection by British forces. It was therefore mandatory to transfer the activities of HEMED to new sites in Jerusalem. On March 17, 1948, the Schneller Complex[19] was transferred from British forces to the Haganah (with the assistance of a bribe).

Tuvia Bar-Ilan—the son of Meir Bar-Ilan, one of the leaders of the Mizrachi religious Zionist party—was appointed commander of HEMED Jerusalem. Tuvia Bar-Ilan was a major in the British Army (Picture 48) and returned to Jerusalem in February 1948 after completing his scientific work on plastic materials at the Brooklyn Polytechnic Institute (46).

Most of the scientists at the Schneller Base (known as HEMED Base No. 2) were chemists such as Heini Eisenberg, Israel Miller (Milo), Yoram Vidor (Avidor), Ora Kedem, and Elisheva Kaufmann. Heini Eisenberg climbed the fence on top

---

19 The Schneller Syrian Orphanage was founded in 1860 by Father Johannes Ludwig Schneller, a Protestant clergyman who came to Jerusalem from Germany.

Picture 48. Tuvia Bar-Ilan, commander of HEMED Jerusalem
(courtesy of Meir Bar-Ilan)

of the Schneller walls and retrieved trip flares[20] installed there by British soldiers. He brought the devices to the workshop of Elik Sochazewer, who copied them and transferred them to Taas for production. Another very important contribution by Heini Eisenberg was the production of cheddite together with Israel Miller (Milo). Israel Milo relates the following story:

> In November 1947, I was asked by Aharon Katchal-sky to join a secret group and to contribute to the security of Israel. My first assignment was to fill shells with TNT. This was done in one of the stables in Beit Hakerem, a suburb of Jerusalem. Dr. Benjamin Kirson, who was one of our inorganic chemistry teachers, joined me. Despite his knowledge of chemistry, he used a mortar to grind perchlorate, phosphorus, and an organic compound. As

---

20 A trip flare is a device used by military forces to secure an area and guard against infiltration. It consists of tripwire around the area, linked to one or more flares.

expected, an explosion occurred and Dr. Kirson was injured. My next assignment was to manufacture cheddite to replace TNT, which was found in Jerusalem only in small quantities. For this we needed potassium chlorate, aluminum powder, and the resin colophonium.

We received the aluminum powder from hardware stores and the colophonium was obtained from carpenters, who used it as a varnish. Together with Heini Eisenberg, we traveled to Potash Industries at the Dead Sea and received large quantities of potassium chloride. After its oxidation by a dangerous process, we obtained potassium perchlorate, which we used for the preparation of cheddite.

With the help of Elik Sochazewer, we established a plant in a laundry in the abandoned suburb of Romema and together with Heini Eisenberg prepared 2,000 kilograms of cheddite. This explosive was used to produce mines and hand grenades. We faced a serious problem: how to keep the explosive dry. At that time we did not have plastic bags, but we found plastic trousers (perhaps from firemen) and thus kept the explosives dry (48, [translated from the Hebrew).

Elisheva Kaufmann (Picture 49) was active in the HEMED base in Jerusalem. She was born in Germany in 1915, immigrated to Palestine in the mid-1930s, and joined Kibbutz Givat Brenner (founded in 1928 in the central district of Israel, located two kilometers south of Rehovot). There, she joined the Haganah and specialized in communication (flag signaling, Morse code, and heliograph, a wireless solar telegraph that sends signals with flashes of sunlight). During her work in agriculture, she met with Dr. Zdenka Samish from the Agricultural Research Station in Rehovot and assisted her in analyzing food products. She moved to Jerusalem in 1945 and began her studies in chemistry at The Hebrew University (49). In November 1947, after the United Nations voted to partition Palestine, she became active in the Haganah and joined the guards protecting Romema. In February 1948, she joined the first military chemistry course, held on the Mount Scopus campus of the university. This course was the beginning of the activities of HEMED.

After completing her training on Mount Scopus, Kaufmann was ordered to work in an isolated building in the Arab village of Lifta, west of Jerusalem. There, she worked with Heini Eisenberg and developed trip flares. In the same building, Dr. Widenfeld produced detonators. Dr. Widenfeld was a chemist who gained considerable experience during her work at Potash Industries at the Dead Sea. She was injured by an unexpected explosion. Kaufmann rushed to provide help.

Picture 49. Elisheva Kaufmann, a pioneer of HEMED, who worked at the Jerusalem base

From Lifta, Kaufmann moved to the WIZO day care center in Beit Hakerem where she, together with Meir Goldman, melted TNT and produced anti-tank mines in wooden frames. Wooden boxes were used because metal containers were not available. This assignment was very urgent, and Goldman, who was religious, agreed to work during the Passover holiday. Every morning Kaufmann and Goldman had to drink milk to counter the toxicity of the TNT. This required a special effort, as milk was a rare commodity in besieged Jerusalem.

The third laboratory was in the Department of Public Health in Machane Yehuda. It was here that Kaufmann conducted chemical analyses in Dr. Gerichter's laboratory. In a similar laboratory, Guta Wertheim was in charge of analyzing the quality of water samples from cisterns in besieged Jerusalem. Wertheim was born in Poland and earned a PhD in microbiology from The Hebrew University in 1951.

The fourth laboratory was near Bikur Cholim Hospital on Strauss Street in the center of Jerusalem. There, Kaufmann was in charge of chemical analyses, together with Renana Ben-Gurion, daughter of Israeli Prime Minister David Ben-Gurion. During her experiments, Kaufmann was injured by an explosion and had to rest for one month. Even Kaufmann, who was a careful and experienced experimental scientist, became the victim of an unexpected explosion. It is also evident that scientific activities in besieged Jerusalem were extremely difficult due to the fact that laboratory space was limited and scientists were forced to move from one place to another until the central HEMED laboratories were established at the Schneller Complex.

In 1949, Kaufmann returned to her studies at The Hebrew University, where she would receive her PhD. Subsequently, she did postdoctoral studies at Mount Sinai Hospital in Chicago and in 1958 was appointed scientist at the Israel Institute for

Biological Research in Ness Ziona. She passed away on January 31, 2015, at the age of one hundred.

Ora Kedem was born in 1924 in Vienna (50). After immigrating to Palestine, she started her studies at The Hebrew University, joined the Haganah, and became a platoon commander. In November 1947, she commanded a unit of the Home Guard (Mishmar Ezrachi) in Jerusalem and subsequently joined HEMED scientists at Mount Scopus. There she produced explosives and Molotov cocktails. When the base at the Schneller Complex was opened, she joined HEMED scientists and continued her activities in research and development. The commander of the base was Tuvia Bar-Ilan. According to her description, he was a professional officer who received his training in the British Army. He was involved in solving military problems and left the administration to Michael Ben-Hanan. Kedem moved from Jerusalem to HEMED Base No.1 and in 1949 became a senior scientist at the Weizmann Institute in Rehovot, where she studied the biological and physical properties of polymers. In 1961, she was awarded the prestigious Israel Prize, together with Aharon Katzir. From 1967 to 1968, she worked at the atomic energy plant in Nahal Soreq, and in 1973 she founded the Department of Membrane Research at the Weizmann Institute. From 1995 to 2003, she continued her research on membranes at Ben-Gurion University of the Negev in Beer-Sheva. Kedem gained international recognition for her research on the use of reverse osmosis for water purification. These studies were based on the use of semi-permeable membranes. She formed an applied research unit with Avishay Braverman. This unit, which was active at Ben-Gurion University, focused its research on water purification.

Arieh Damiel (Schweiger) was enlisted by Abraham Berman in 1947 and was asked to join the team led by Aharon Katchalsky to produce tear gas (51). At the beginning of the War of Independence, he joined fighters in the Old City of Jerusalem. When the HEMED base in the Schneller Complex opened, he joined a group (which included Hayuta Fogel) and produced ignition devices for flame throwers. He continued his studies when he was transferred to HEMED Base No. 1 in Tel Haim.

A. Preparation of the *Conus* in an Attempt to Penetrate into the Old City

One of the major activities of the HEMED base in Jerusalem was the preparation of the "Big *Conus*." On July 17, 1948, David Shaltiel, the commander of the Jerusalem district, summoned his officers and disclosed that on Friday, July 18, an attempt would be made to penetrate into the Old City, which was occupied by Palestinians. The operation was called *Kedem* ("East") and two regiments were assigned to attack. The Beit Horon regiment, under the command of Meir Zorea, was supposed to attack from Mount Zion, the southern wall of the Old City. A regiment manned by members of the Irgun was supposed to attack from the north, facing the New Gate, while a Lehi[21] group was supposed to attack from the west between the Jaffa Gate and Mount Zion (Picture 50).

The Beit Horon regiment commenced its attack from Yemin Moshe and the fighters climbed up Mount Zion, carrying with them a heavy, cone-shaped bomb called the "Big *Conus*," which was supposed to pierce a hole in the wall of the Old City (Picture 50) by exploding its hollow charge near the Zion Gate.

---

21 Lehi, acronym for the Fighters for the Freedom of Israel, was commonly referred to in English as the Stern Gang.

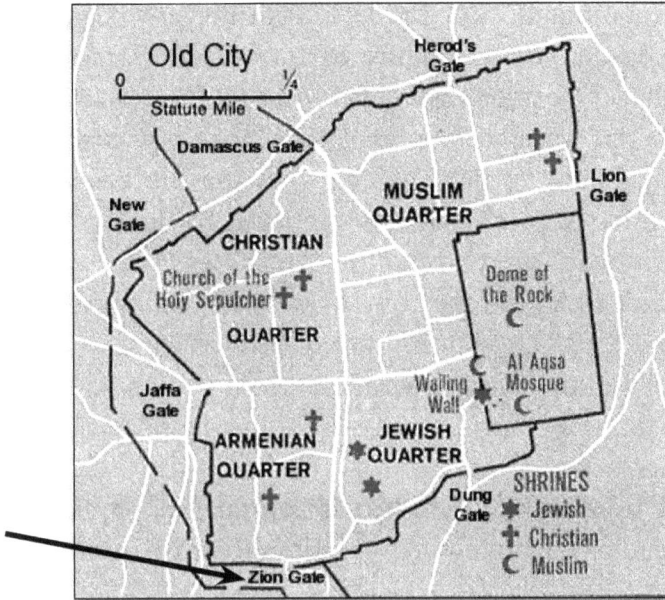

Picture 50. Map of the Old City of Jerusalem
(the arrow indicates the site of the explosion).

The bomb weighed approximately 300 kilograms and the soldiers had to divide it into parts and carry them up Mount Zion. They then had to assemble the parts, which took time. At 3:00 a.m. the Big *Conus* was ready, and at 5:00 a.m. soldiers placed it near the walls of the Old City. There was a powerful explosion, but the wall wasn't penetrated (53).

Lehi fighters were supplied with two similar bombs. A car carrying one of the bombs was hit by a shell fired by Arabs stationed on the walls of the Old City. An explosion occurred and the bomb was hit. The Lehi fighters approached the wall and placed the second bomb there. Again, this explosion was not successful and the wall was only charred (54). In the meantime, fighters from an Irgun regiment succeeded in conquering the New Gate and advanced into the Old City. However, they had to retreat as they didn't receive support from the attackers from the south and the west (53).

The commanders of the Jerusalem Brigade began to discuss the reasons for the failure of the attack. Some of them claimed that the explosives loaded into the Big *Conus* were defective, so the waves of the explosion were not concentrated into a single spot. Others claimed that the Big *Conus* lacked a "liner," a metal piece that was supposed to shield the top of the explosives. It appeared that the "liner" was not essential, as the anti-tank PIAT did not contain a "liner" and was still effective as an anti-tank weapon. Indeed, Prof. Racah, who copied models for hollow-charged weapons from Italian sources, did not insist that the "liner" was essential for the operation of the armament.

Igal Talmi, a distinguished Israeli nuclear physicist, who was the head of the hollow charge unit in Rehovot, explains (55):

> Prof. Racah met an Italian scientist named Segeri, who was engaged in hollow charge research in Italy. He brought with him some magazines in which weapons containing hollow-charged explosives were described. In the meantime, Jenka Ratner supplied us with information he obtained during his service in the British Navy. He even gave us an incorrect drawing describing the structure of a hollow-charged shell. A paper published in the *Journal of Applied Physics* gave us a correct mathematical and physical description of hollow-charged weapons. This information was very useful and served the group headed by Talmi, which included Uri Habersheim, Shula Kogan, Abraham Huss, Hannah Goldring, and Shneor Lipson of the Weizmann Institute. When the army approached us and asked us to conceive the absurd idea of piercing a hole into the thick wall of the Old City, we planned to manufacture a "big *conus*." We prepared such an explosive and tested it in a quarry at the Castel near Jerusalem. The field experiment was successful and a two-meter-deep

hole was formed. We planned to widen the hole by means of a second explosion of a "sausage" placed in the hole. The initiative to produce the *conus* came from T. Bar-Ilan, the commander of the Jerusalem base. Moshe Dayan [...] did not know about the *conus* and planned to place explosives in a sewer tunnel under the walls of the Old City. This was indeed done, but the charge was exploded only after the end of the War of Independence [Picture 51]. [translated from the Hebrew]

Picture 51. Exploding a charge in a sewer tunnel under the walls of the Old City (after the end of the War of Independence).

There were many discussions on the role of a "liner" in improving the blast of the hollow charge. Some claimed that they found fragments of aluminum or copper layers on the top of a steel plate that was treated by a hollow charge explosive. On the other hand, Igal Talmi and his group found that a hollow charge could operate without a "liner," but the type of explosion was different. Instead of having a clear hole, a "crater" was formed on the top of the steel block that served as the target of the charge.

I believe that there is a difference between using hollow charges as anti-tank weapons and using them for piercing a hole in a wall. For anti-tank purposes, a direct and a focused blast is needed. In this case a "liner" is beneficial. On the other hand, if the hollow charge is needed to act as a blast, a "liner" is not essential. I believe that the failure of the "Big *Conus*" in piercing a hole in the wall of the Old City was due to it being placed on the wrong site. Examination of the site where the charge was placed revealed that it was placed on the ground near the wall, while on the other side of the wall (inside the Old City) the level of the ground was much higher, so that the blast was arrested. This theory is supported by a story told by Elik Sochazewer to Ezra Greenberg (56):

> I met an engineer named Zarkin in the presence of Gil Gilevich, who was the city engineer of the municipality of Jerusalem. He told me that we knew about the plan to put the "Big *Conus*" near the wall of the Old City in a place called the Armenian Court. At this site, the ground within the Old City was approximately two meters higher than that on the outer site of the wall. Gilevich claimed that the "Big *Conus*" should have been placed between the Zion Gate and the Dung Gate, where the wall of the Old City is only 30 to 40 centimeters thick. Even a small amount of explosives could lead to the collapse of the wall, so that even a vehicle could pass through.

> I was asked by the Scientific Council to prepare five to seven "big *conuses*." I received the drawings from Prof. Racah, but I claimed that even if the charge did explode, only a small hole would be formed, and [it] would not permit the passage of soldiers. To enlarge the hole, it should be cooled with water and then filled with a new batch of explosives, which should then widen the hole. But I did what I was ordered to do. So, I went to the workshop of a welder and brought with me 14-millimeter-thick steel

plates. In those days electricity was often disrupted, so we had to go to the Jewish Agency offices, where electricity was supplied by a generator. We rushed and on the same day several "big *conuses*" were ready. We took them to Beit Hakerem to the WIZO day care center, where the explosive was melted and poured into the empty shells. Benny Marshak, a senior Palmach officer, came with a car and took two *conuses*. The melted explosive was still warm (40°C), but we carried the shells in a ditch near St. John Eye Hospital up to Mount Zion. As you know, the shells were placed near the walls of the Old City. The explosion was not successful and resulted in only a small charred hole. [translated from the Hebrew]

It is very likely that if the "big *conus*" had been placed at a higher level (on a ladder) or at another site along the wall, the results would have been better. Reuven Eshel claimed that the "*conus*" should not have been attached to the wall, but rather placed several meters away to increase the power of the blast (28).

B. Collaboration between HEMED and Israel Military Industries (Taas)

Israel Military Industries Ltd. (known by the Hebrew acronym "Taas" and in English "IMI") was a leader in the design and development of innovative military defense systems. The collaboration between HEMED and Taas was extremely important in saving besieged Jerusalem. Due to these joint efforts, explosives, mines, Molotov cocktails, and bombs were produced in Jerusalem and supported fighters. In Jerusalem, until March 1948, two thousand anti-personnel mines, two thousand anti-tank mines, and three thousand Molotov cocktails were produced. There is no doubt that these devices saved Jerusalem. In other regions of Israel, this collaboration was not so fruitful.

The initiative for this collaboration came from the leaders of HEMED. As Joseph Evron explained, "Until December 1947, Taas did not exist in Jerusalem. Elik Sochazewer did some experiments at the workshop of The Hebrew University and initiated the formation of a branch of Taas in Jerusalem" (57).

At the end of 1947, Aharon Katchalsky and Elik Sochazewer created small units responsible for the production of chemicals and small numbers of land mines. In January 1948, the command of the Haganah in Jerusalem decided to establish an independent branch of Taas. The leaders of this branch were Aharon Katchalsky, who had the vision and scientific background, and Elik Sochazewer, who was in charge of production. Yehiel Ben Zeev was appointed production officer. This is his story:

> At the beginning, the high command of the Haganah did not recommend the formation of a separate unit of Taas in Jerusalem and this new organization was not supported financially. However, we were under the command of the Haganah in Jerusalem and received instructions from their officers. Loans from public and private sources solved some of our financial problems. Ben-Gurion, as head of the Jewish Agency, gave us a single donation of 2,000 pounds, which was a substantial amount in those days.

> In Jerusalem there was an urgent need for explosives, including detonators. To solve these problems, new production plants were required. Obviously, new sources were needed to open these plants. So we approached Yigael Yadin, an Israeli archaeologist, politician, and the second chief of staff of the Israel Defense Forces, and requested his support. He realized that our requests were reasonable and discussed them at the general meeting of the chief of staff. Some members of the staff did not like the idea of having a separate industry in Jerusalem. However, Yadin

succeeded in convincing them and from that day on we received support from the Ministry of Defense.

After receiving the necessary support, we started to organize Taas in Jerusalem. Some volunteers joined us and we began the production of explosives in private workshops and at the Brandeis School of Fine Mechanics. When the production load increased, we moved to abandoned houses, organized a transportation system, and started to produce explosives, detonators, land mines, and shells in larger quantities. Subsequently, we constructed a plant to fill mines and shells with explosives in Beit Hakerem, a suburb of Jerusalem. In Romema we built a plant for the production of detonators, fuses for hand grenades, and flares. In Jerusalem, we could not produce heavy arms. These had to be brought to the city by light Primus planes. One day we heard that in Tel Aviv a new heavy mortar called "Davidka" had been invented. We asked to receive two samples at our base in Kiryat Anavim (the first kibbutz on the highland near Jerusalem), so that they could be tested and possibly also copied.

All credit has to be given to Elik Sochazewer, who copied the mortar and even upgraded it. For the production of the Davidka, we needed pipes, which we retrieved from sewage plants and water supplies. We even confiscated a canon, a souvenir from World War I, which was placed in the Menora Officers' Club Museum. After extensive efforts and round-the-clock work, we produced fifteen Davidka mortar along with several thousands of shells. This new supply of heavy arms contributed much to the defense of Jerusalem.

Many scientists with academic backgrounds were available in Jerusalem. On the other hand, technicians with mechanical skills existed only in small numbers. In

Jerusalem, foundries that could melt iron did not exist. Only foundries that could melt aluminum (at a lower temperature) operated in the Machane Yehuda market. Flares were copied and manufactured.

Throughout the War of Independence there was close collaboration between HEMED and Taas in Jerusalem. This resulted in the production of newly invented weapons and the improvement of those produced by others, mainly thanks to Aharon Katchalsky and Elik Sochazewer, who complemented one another. One had the theoretical background, while the other had profound technical knowledge. In other parts of the country the two bodies did not collaborate and very often competition hampered progress.

When the scope of Taas increased, additional sites for production were needed and a temporary building was constructed near the former German Consulate and engines were transferred to this new site (57, translated from the Hebrew).

Jenka Ratner, who served in both Taas and HEMED, designed and produced a six-inch mortar with a range of 3,000 meters. This mortar was used successfully in the attack of Iraq Suidan on November 9, 1948.

The "Davidka" was a heavy weapon that was used successfully in the attacks on Safed in the Upper Galilee and Abu Tor on the outskirts of Jerusalem. This mortar was developed neither by Taas nor by HEMED, but rather by David Leibovich, a teacher from the agricultural school of Mikveh Israel (Picture 52.) At the beginning of the War of Independence, the Technical Department of the Palmach developed a small mortar called *Parosh* ("Flea"), which could fire a 15-kilogram shell a distance of 400 meters.

Picture 52. The "Davidka"

CHAPTER 9:

HEMED BASE NO. 3 IN HAIFA AND CURDANI

At the Technion in Haifa, there were many engineers and scientists who contributed to military sciences even before Israel declared independence. Dr. Torecki improved the production of Molotov cocktails and Prof. Yohanan Ratner was a leading figure in designing and producing new weapons. He was one of the founders of HEMED and continued his activities until he was appointed ambassador to the Soviet Union. Prof. Markus Reiner, a well-known expert on the flow of liquids, and Prof. Hugo Heimann, from the Chemical Engineering Department at the Technion, contributed much to the development and production of arms. When Abraham Berman planned the operations of HEMED on April 4, 1948, Moshe Ish-Shalom from the Israel Ceramic and Silicate Institute at the Technion was appointed commander of HEMED Haifa. The research officer of that base was Naftali Steiner. On May 1, 1948, thirty-three scientists were working at this base (58). Subsequently, scientists and engineers moved from HEMED Base No. 1 to Haifa in order to increase manpower.

When the base in Curdani opened, many scientists from the Technion decided to move to the new site, which promised more space and better facilities. Together with scientists and engineers from the Technion, scientists from other HEMED bases joined those who moved to Curdani. Among them was Jenka Ratner, who moved from HEMED Base No. 1 and brought with him a number of enthusiastic scientists. He was very productive and was twice awarded an Israel Security Prize. Ratner designed and produced a recoilless gun and was promoted to the rank of colonel. In the mid-1950s, he developed the super-bazooka, a man-portable recoilless rocket anti-tank weapon. The development of this weapon lasted for three years. Moshe (Moja) Epstein was also one of the engineers who moved from HEMED Base No. 1 to Curdani, where he laid the foundations for the construction of different rockets. In 1968, Rafael, the Armament Development Authority, was formed and gained international recognition and respect. In 2006, Rafael sold rockets and weapons, devices that were first designed in HEMED, worth $1 billion (59). Yehuda Venezia aptly noted (16) that David Ben-Gurion always claimed that Israelis should design and produce their own weapons rather than purchase them from other armies. At HEMED Base No. 1, the motto was "What other countries can do, we can do better." Indeed, when some experts came from Czechoslovakia to "teach" us how to develop incendiary bombs, they had problems igniting the material. We used our own technologies and helped them to start the fire. We could certainly conclude that our knowledge was better than that of the foreign experts.

CHAPTER 10:

PHYSICISTS AT HEMED BASE NO. 4

In a letter Aharon Katchalsky wrote to his brother Ephraim, he said that on Mount Scopus, a group of physicists was working parallel to a group of chemists to develop new weapons. This group of physicists was under the command of Prof. Giulio Racah, who was born on February 9, 1909, in Florence. He was a well-known Israeli Italian physicist and mathematician who passed away on August 28, 1965, in Florence, apparently poisoned by gas in his bathroom.

Another member of the group was Prof. Samuel Sambursky, head of the Department of Physics at The Hebrew University. In 1942, Sambursky was appointed by the British Mandatory government to set up a board of scientific and idustrial research. In this capacity, he developed optical instruments, which helped the war effort during World War II. When the Security Council was established by the Haganah in 1947, Sambursky was invited to be a member. Heini Fry, who completed his doctoral training in Vienna, worked under Sambursky in the Department of Physics and also became a member of the Security Council. After the formation of HEMED, Fry became the commander of the Physical Unit in Rehovot. He, his wife Yael Rosenfeld, and Dr. Israel Meibom developed optical instruments to use moonlight for night surveillance.

Gideon Yekutieli explained in his book (in Hebrew) *The Days of HEMED* that a group of physicists was formed by the Haganah as early as 1946. The group included Amos De Shalit, who achieved prominence in the field of nuclear physics and who has been a key figure in the development of science in Israel. Aharon Donagi was the coordinator of the group. According to Yekutieli (60):

> In February 1948, the group of physicists started to work on Mount Scopus. Prof. Racah conceived the idea that hollow charge explosives should be developed. He inspired Amos De Shalit, Uri Habersheim, Gvirol Goldring, and Gideon Yekutieli to work on this subject. The group of physicists moved to HEMED Base No. 1 and continued to work on hollow-charged explosives. In Givat Haim, the group included Uri Habersheim, Dalia Carmi, Abraham Huss, Hannah Cohen and Shula Kogan. In July 1948, Igal Talmi joined the group and became its commander.

Igal Talmi was born in Kfar Yehezkel, a *moshav ovdim*[22] in the Jezreel Valley, where his parents were school teachers (55). He studied at the elementary school in his moshav, continued his studies at the high school in Kibbutz Geva, and finally at Herzliya High School in Tel Aviv. After graduating, he joined the Palmach and was trained at Kibbutz Tel Joseph. After completing his service in the Palmach, he enrolled at The Hebrew University where he majored in physics and minored in mathematics and philosophy.

---

22 A *moshav ovdim* is a workers' settlement of small holders with independent, but cooperative, farm units.

In 1947, he completed his studies at the university and joined the Michmash Regiment in the Jerusalem Hish (Field Corps).[23] He fought in battles in Neveh Yaakov and heard about the formation of HEMED, but Talmi preferred to remain in a combat unit, realizing that he was needed there, as many of his comrades were wounded or even fell on the battlefield. In April 1948, Aharon Katchalsky convinced him to leave the combat unit and join HEMED (Picture 53).

Avraham Kogan, another physicist, developed land mines in the form of pebbles (*bebalach*). If I am not mistaken, they were used to block the road near Beit Guvrin. Other physicists developed "igniting leaves," which were supposed to be ignited by sunlight.

The electronic unit included Heini Fry and Israel Pelach, who later became the director of the Soreq Nuclear Research Center. They developed optical devices that used moonlight for night surveillance. Benjamin Fraenkel used infrared beams for a similar purpose. Other physicists joined mechanical engineers to develop two- and three-inch anti-tank cannons (M-2 and M-3).

Gvirol Goldring was injured in a field test near Nebi Rubin (61). He claimed that there were problems in firing shells from the M-2 weapon and it was not certain where the shells exploded. It was decided to send an "observer" to detect the hit site. Goldring was sent on that mission. Unfortunately, the shell hit the ground near Goldring and he was wounded.

The physicists also developed recoilless guns and Gvirol Goldring was asked to demonstrate their activity in the presence of General Yigael Yadin. To demonstrate that the gun did not recoil, it was attached to a rope, which was tied to a tree. When a shell was fired from the gun, it did not, in fact, recoil,

---

23 The Hish (Field Corps) was a corps formed by the Haganah during the British Mandate.

but rather exploded. Fortunately, nobody was hurt. The development of recoilless guns was completed only three years later by Moshe (Moja) Epstein, who worked in Curdani.

Picture 53. Physicists in a jeep. Gideon Yekutieli is in the passenger seat; Igal Talmi is in the back.

I remember that the physicists also developed a remote control vehicle. Indeed, Ephraim Katzir noted that "Fry constructed a vehicle operated by batteries that was guided by a rope. We called it 'the dog' (62). Very often it would return to Fry and hit him rather than reaching the target." A similar "dog" was apparently prepared by Prof. A. Bonfiglioli from the Technion in Haifa. He planned to use it to destroy an Arab stronghold in his town, but the plan never came to fruition.

Extensive research in military chemistry was also conducted at the Weizmann Institute in Rehovot, mainly in the Sieff Institute. This activity was not approved by Chaim Weizmann, who did not like the idea that military-oriented research would be carried out in his institute, which was designed to help humanity. The military-oriented research was under the supervision of E.D. Bergmann, who returned to Israel in March 1948.

According to Uri Littauer (41), most of the research at HEMED Base No.1 was focused on solving chemical problems. When physicists planned to solve problems in the field of physics, the equipment at the Tel Haim base was not sufficient. Since more sophisticated equipment was available in the Sieff Institute, many physicists moved to Rehovot to continue their experiments. There they studied the velocities of bullets and the actions of explosives and began to develop rockets. Uri Littauer, together with Israel Miller, prepared a solid-based propellant designed for rockets. This study was discontinued when Hayuta Vogel was injured while taking part in an experiment. Several years later, Uri Littauer visited the Rafael Institute in Curdani and found out that they had developed a solid-based propellant similar to the one he had prepared in Rehovot in 1948.

Ben-Gurion was influenced by E.D. Bergmann, and in 1949 he provided six fellowships to students of physics who had graduated from The Hebrew University and served in HEMED. They were supposed to work for advanced training in nuclear physics in the best laboratories in the world. Prof. Racah of The Hebrew University, the only Israeli leader in theoretical physics, used his contacts with various leading scientists worldwide to place the Israeli physicists in the best laboratories. Amos De Shalit and Igal Talmi were sent to Eidgenössische Technische Hochschule Zürich (ETH) under the guidance of Paul Scherrer, professor of experimental physics, and Wolfgang Pauli, professor of theoretical physics. Uri Habersheim was sent to the University of Chicago where Prof. Enrico Fermi worked. Gideon Yekutieli was sent to Bristol to work under the guidance of Prof. M. Pavel, Gvirol Goldring went to the Department of Experimental Physics at the Imperial College in London, and Israel Pelach was sent to the University of Amsterdam in the Netherlands (63).

When they returned to Israel upon completion of their advanced training, they decided to leave the Army to work in academic research, so that the results of their studies could be published. Only Israel Pelach decided to continue his activities in the Department of Defense and became director of the Soreq Nuclear Research Center. The others applied for positions at the Weizmann Institute in Rehovot and their applications were approved by Moshe Sharett, whereas Shimon Peres objected. Finally, Ben-Gurion and Ephraim Katzir supported them and on January 20, 1954, an agreement was signed between Shimon Peres, the director general of the Department of Defense, and Mr. Meyer Weisgal, the first chancellor of the Weizmann Institute. According to the agreement, Weisgal would pay a half million pounds to the Department of Defense, so that HEMED Base No. 4 could be transferred to the Weizmann Institute with its equipment and scientists. In May 1954, the new Department of Nuclear Physics was opened at the Weizmann Institute and Amos De Shalit was appointed its head (63).

CHAPTER 11:

OPERATION UNITS

A. Unit Commanders

The British military research and development departments conducted research but did not have operation units
that could apply the results of their research to the battlefield.
As many of the scientists of HEMED served in combat units
and had military experience, it was decided to create operation units for the different sections of HEMED. The different sections were HEMED A, HEMED B, and HEMED C.
HEMED A dealt with chemical problems, HEMED B conducted research in the field of biological defense and warfare,
while HEMED C was engaged in solving problems in geology
and nuclear research. It should be noted that similar operation
units did not exist in any other army. Who were the commanders of the operation units?

AHARON DONAGI

Aharon Donagi, who changed his name from Wax, left
high school and joined Company H of the Palmach in 1943 (64).
In 1945, he was asked by David Shaltiel, an Israeli military and

intelligence officer, to become an assistant in the scientific department of the Haganah. He was arrested by the British on "Black Sabbath," on June 29, 1946. After being imprisoned in Latrun for two months, he resumed his activities in the Haganah and attempted to develop new arms. One example of these was a flame thrower, which he developed together with Abraham Berman. Donagi also recruited physicists Amos De Shalit and Gideon Yekuteili and asked them to plan a "theoretical approach" for the production of rockets. In Kibbutz Givat Hashlosha, Donagi had an illegal storage place for hand grenades. He asked the physicists to study the velocity of explosions. Donagi (also called "Aharonchik"; see Chapter 6) was appointed commander of the operation units and took part in attacking the stronghold of Iraq Suidan. He also supervised Yehuda Venezia, who was a demolition expert in the Palmach.

ZVI PELACH (PALCHOVIC)

Zvi Pelach (Picture 54) joined Onn Company on February 2, 1948, and took part in the military chemistry course on Mount Scopus. After completing his training, he was asked by Amos Chorev to teach mining and demolition to Palmach fighters stationed in Kiryat Anavim and Kalia. He also instructed members of the Palyam, naval commandos, in the use of explosives and pyrotechnical weapons. He and his brother, Israel, left Jerusalem in the last convoy to leave the city and moved to HEMED Base No.1 in Tel Haim. There, he joined the operation units, was appointed deputy commander, and assisted Aharon Strikovsky (Nir) in designing "heavy mortars." When Strikovsky left HEMED, Zvi Pelach remained the only expert in the design and use of "heavy mortars." One of them was a six-inch mortar, which he describes in the following passage:

Picture 54. Zvi Pelach (during operations)

The mortar consisted of a welded steel barrel, six inches in diameter. A steel wire and some bolts were used to strengthen the structure. At the end of steel barrel, there was a bridge block into which the propellant was inserted. The shell was very heavy (more than 40 kilograms) and contained TNT. The range of the mortar was about 2,000 meters and the explosion of the shell produced a frightening noise. The major problem of this weapon was the uncertainty of the fate of the shell after it was fired. It could explode in the barrel, or in the vicinity of the shooting squad, or, with luck, reach the target. Therefore, we decided to fire the mortar from a ditch using a long cable.

We conducted the first experiments near the Sharon Hotel in Herzliya, shooting into the Mediterranean. This was our base and practically the first artillery base of the Israeli Defense Forces. This mortar, or our "heavy artillery," as we called it, contributed much to our war efforts. It was used by Yitzhak Sadeh and his troops in their attempts to conquer the stronghold Iraq Suidan, which blocked the road to the Negev (the southern part of the country). In fact, we placed two mortars in Kibbutz Negba and tried to shoot horizontally, like a canon. I believe that this was the only time a shell was fired from a mortar horizontally. The distance from the target was approximately 1,700 meters. Luckily, all the shells hit the target. We also used an M-2 canon, placed on a jeep (34).

I was asked by Oded Messer, operation officer of Yitzhak Sadeh, to bring our M-2 mortars to another battlefield, Iraq al-Manshiyya. We fired several shells from this canon, which had a barrel made from a train wagon axle. This weapon was quite effective. It was not heavy and could be carried by hand, unlike the M-3, which was heavy and dangerous. Injuries to the hands of the shooter were another disadvantage of the M-3. When Daniel Halevy, a gifted mathematician, used the M-3 gun, an explosion occurred and he was seriously injured.

After the war, I wanted to leave military activities and return to an academic unit. My request to work at the Weizmann Institute was approved and I started to work toward my MSc under the guidance of E.D. Bergmann. This took only three months, after which I returned to HEMED Base No. 1 and joined the group headed by Dr. Ephraim Levkovich to study the properties of liquid explosives. I tried to mix two inert ingredients to form a potent explosive.

On April 22, 1951, I attempted to measure the velocity of an explosion wave. To do this, I had to insert the detonator into a vessel containing the explosive. An explosion occurred when I was holding the detonator in my hand. Apparently, I pulled the electrical cable by mistake. This resulted in me damaging my fingers, getting a splinter in my left eye, and sustaining many injuries to my body. Yeshayahu Gallili took me to the hospital and I will never forget this. Even before that event, I had regarded him as a brave and generous man who deserved admiration. I stayed in the hospital for seven months and they wanted to amputate my hand. I refused but I was operated on five times.

At the end of 1951, I left the hospital, returned to HEMED, and met with E.D. Bergmann, who had left the Weizmann Institute and become the head of the Scientific Department of HEMED. I was determined to leave my work in the field of chemistry and become an accountant as I had to do when I graduated high school. Bergmann did not like that idea and suggested that I should return to science and work for my doctorate. I said, "How can I do this? I cannot move my hand." He said, "Do not worry. I will give you a technician." The technician was B. Peskin, with whom I started my PhD dissertation in 1952. I worked around the clock, from 8:00 a.m. until midnight. After a year and half, I finished my dissertation, and then took a vacation, which I spent in Europe. When I returned to HEMED, I was discharged from the IDF with the rank of captain. Bergmann asked me to become the scientific director of HEMED Base No. 1, after the retirement of Aviv Peleg (Feldbrovsky). I served in this capacity for a year and a half, even when HEMED was transferred from the Army to the Ministry of Defense. During this time, I was appointed chairperson of the group that dealt with protection against poisonous gases and subsequently I became a member of the office of the chief scientist of the Ministry of Defense (34, translated from the Hebrew).

After completing his duties in military research and development, Pelach fulfilled central functions at Ben-Gurion University of the Negev in Beer-Sheva.

MICHAEL BEN-HANAN (ZEMEL)

Michael Ben-Hanan was born in 1912 and grew up in Halberstadt, Germany, where his parents, who had emigrated from Kalish, Poland, had a farm (65). Since childhood, Ben-Hanan had liked gymnastics and specialized in floor exercises. After graduating from high school, he moved to Frankfurt and studied mathematics, physics, and physical education. This was a rare combination at the time. In 1933, when the Nazi regime took over, Ben-Hanan immigrated to Palestine, where he lived with his uncle in Nahalal (a collective settlement in northern Israel). Subsequently, he moved to Jerusalem, where he joined the Haganah and accepted responsibility for organizing secret illegal weapon storage. When he became a Haganah course instructor, he met his future wife, Sarah Abutbul, a descendent of a prominent family from Safed. During the Arab uprising from 1936 to 1939, he moved to the Dead Sea and became the commander of Kibbutz Kalia.

When he returned to Jerusalem, he continued his activities in the Haganah, but he also taught physics and mathematics at Gymnasia Haivrit High School. Among his students were the brothers Aharon and Ephraim Katchalsky, who asked him to join HEMED when the War of Independence broke out. Ben-Hanan started to work toward his PhD, but his studies were interrupted by his activities during the war.

In 1945, he changed his name from Zemel to Ben-Hanan and became famous because of his physical fitness instructions, which were broadcast on the radio. When his son, Yossi Ben-Hanan, returned to Israel from a trip to the Far East and joined the fighters in the Golan Heights during the Yom Kippur War, it was said in code that "the son of the physical instructor has arrived."

Michael Ben-Hanan joined HEMED and was in charge of the maintenance of the Jerusalem base. In July 1948, he moved to HEMED Base No. 1 and was appointed one of the commanders of the operation units (Picture 55).

Picture 55. Michael Ben-Hanan firing a shell from a Davidka in Jerusalem (courtesy of Yossi Ben-Hanan).

After the War of Independence, Ben-Hanan remained in the Army and was the deputy regiment commander of Jerusalem Brigade No. 16. After completing his military service, he became a tour guide and regarded this as a mission. He passed away in 2001, having earned the respect of many who appreciated his praiseworthy activities.

B. The Involvement of HEMED in the Battles of Iraq Suidan

The battle of Iraq Suidan was described by Netanel Lorch (66, translated from the Hebrew) as follows:

We called the police station of Iraq Suidan the "Monster on the Hill" [Picture 56]. It was evacuated by the British Police forces and handed over to the Muslim

Brotherhood. Because this monster blocked the way to the southern Negev, several attempts were made to conquer it. On the nights of May 18 and 17, 1948, two attempts were made to attack the fortress. They failed, as the Egyptians used flares to illuminate the area. A third attack also failed. In the first stage of the attack, a demolition squad reached the first barbed wire fence surrounding the building and succeeded in dismantling a dangerous mine. When they tried to advance, they were discovered by the Egyptian defenders, who opened heavy fire. Our soldiers arrived at the second fence and demolished it. Another unit succeeded in reaching the third fence and two of them were wounded.

Picture 56. The police station of Iraq Suidan

Breaking the fourth fence resulted in the wounding of another Israeli soldier. In the meantime, the Egyptians used flares, which made the attack more difficult. Unexpectedly, there was a fifth fence, which was finally blown up and the attackers reached the gate of the police station. The time passed rapidly and it was dawn. There was no chance of finishing the attack in daylight, and the troops had to retreat.

The fifth attack was launched on October 19, following heavy artillery bombardments. The Egyptians were waiting for the attackers and threw hand grenades at the advancing soldiers. This attack also failed. Some positions west of Iraq Suidan were conquered by soldiers of the Givati Brigade and several secret documents were detected and deciphered. It turned out that Iraq Suidan was defended by a company of elite forces and not by several untrained soldiers.

It was therefore decided that the next attack should be started from the west, which was apparently less fortified, as it was close to other Egyptian positions, which we had taken.

The attack was started in the evening, by bombing from airplanes, using heavy artillery and three *Paroshim* ("Fleas," miniatures of the Davidka mortars). At this time, the demolition squad advanced close to the fence, in an armored car. They were supposed to blow up the fence and planned to use flame throwers to repel the Egyptian defenders. After this, according to the plan, a truck loaded with explosives would be driven close to the wall of the fortress and it was hoped that after an explosion, a hole would be made in the wall.

The bombing from the air started at 18:00, but the arrival of the troops was delayed and the artillery started to fire only after midnight. The fence was not reached and the flame throwers were far outside of effective range, which would have been less than 120 meters. The truck loaded with explosives attempted to approach the wall of the fortress. Unfortunately, the truck was hit by a PIAT shell and the driver and the demolition squad were injured and jumped into a ditch. They were saved. Then the explosives in the truck exploded, but since they were 30 meters away from the wall, no damage was caused. However, the fences around the building were damaged. This provided an opportunity for another demolition squad to approach the western entrance of the building and place explosives near the door. In fact, this was the first time that Israeli soldiers had come close to the wall of the building. The explosives shattered the entrance of the building and four soldiers tried to break through the damaged entrance. Only the platoon commander made it, but he was wounded by the splinters of a hand grenade. It was the end of the night and all the troops retreated (67).

All the previous attacks had taken place at night to conceal the site of the attack. But these plans failed, as the start of artillery fire indicated the beginning of the attack. Moreover, the use of flares permitted the detection of the attackers even at night. Yitzhak Sadeh suggested changing the plan of operation and attacking during the day. This time, heavy artillery should be used to repel the Egyptian soldiers from their positions. The Beit Guvrin police station, which was similar to that of Iraq Suidan, was used as a model and permitted the training of the attackers. The attack was planned to start on the afternoon of November 9, 1948, with the hope that the setting sun would blind the Egyptian defenders (68).

A regiment of the armored corps was assigned for the attack, which was started by heavy artillery and mortar shootings. According to the plan, the attack would be started by an infantry company, transported on half-truck vehicles. These would be accompanied by two tanks carrying demolition experts with their explosives. Should the first stage fail, a second unit armed with flame throwers would replace them. In case of difficulties, a third stage would start at night.

On the morning of November 9, the attack began, with sporadic shooting at the target to test the accuracy of the weapons. At 14:00, heavy bombardment began.

Yitzhak Sadeh said, "The music of the orchestra had started; all the guns began shooting. We were somewhat nervous; some shells exploded near the police station and did not hit the target. Now the 'sweet baby' [the name of the secret weapon] started shooting, but the first shells exploded far away from the target. But then a shell hit the ceiling of the fortress and another exploded near the entrance of the fortress in the direction of Kibbutz Negba. The whole area was covered with heavy smoke."

At around 15:00 p.m., Egyptian soldiers started to escape from the police station in an attempt to reach the nearby Arab village of Iraq Suidan. In the meantime, the fire continued and the Egyptian flag that had been placed on the southeast tower of the fortress disappeared at 15:47, apparently knocked down by an exploding shell.

The final attack began at 16:00. Infantry carried on half-trucks accompanied by the two tanks approached the target. The barbed wire fence was demolished. Explosives were placed near the wall of the target. Following an explosion, our soldiers penetrated into the fortress through the hole formed by the explosion. The attack was soon completed and the Egyptian soldiers surrendered (68). During this attack, our forces did not lose a single soldier.

This is the summary of the battle as reported by Netanel Lorch (66, translated from Hebrew):

Yeruham Cohen reported (69): "Yitzhak Rabin, Yigal Allon and myself climbed on a jeep and after a short while we reached the police station, surrounded by celebrating

Israeli soldiers. The occupied fortress was full of stinking and burning gun powder smoke."

I took part in the attack on Iraq Suidan as a member of the HEMED operation units. Zvi Pelach was the commander and other members of the unit were Michael Ben-Hanan, Aharon Donagi, and Shlomo Gur (Grezovsky). We arrived at Kibbutz Negba with six-inch mortars equipped with 45-kilogram shells. The range of the mortar was approximately 2,000 meters. After placing the mortars in trenches, we waited until the afternoon, when the attack started. I was asked to climb to the top of the water tower of the kibbutz and report the fate of the fired shells (Picture 57).

Picture 57. The water tower of Kibbutz Negba with damage sustained from shells fired from Iraq Suidan

From the top of the water tower, I could watch the progress of the attack. At the beginning our mortar shells hit the ground near the fortress, but then one shell exploded on the roof of the fortress and the western gate of the police station was shattered. From my observation point, I saw all this and also the Egyptian flag being hit on the top of one of the police towers. Next, I saw a half-truck advancing toward the wall of the police station from the west. A demolition squad placed explosives near the wall and after the explosion resulted in an opening in the wall, soldiers moved through it into the fortress.

One could ask whether the operation units of HEMED contributed to the conquest of Iraq Suidan. If so, what was its contribution? From the operations described above, it is clear that the police station was protected by a well-trained elite Egyptian company. It is also evident that seven attempts to conquer the fortress by the Palmach, paratroopers, Givati Brigade soldiers, and armored corps all failed in their mission. Perhaps a change in tactics—attacking during daylight and not at night, led to the operation's success. HEMED contributed to the success by supplying flame throwers, *Paroshim*, and heavy mortars and their shells.

Picture 58 shows the damage caused by the shell that hit the police station. Other shells succeeded in hitting the roof of the police station, penetrating into the building, and finally breaking and opening the entrance gate of the fortress. We can conclude that HEMED fulfilled an important role in conquering one of the most important and fortified positions of the War of Independence.

Picture 59 shows Kibbutz Negba in the center of the map. The water tower is a round circle in the middle of the kibbutz. On the right (the east) there is a military cemetery, in which the bodies of soldiers who defended the kibbutz were buried. At the bottom of the map, south of Route 35, there is a settlement,

Picture 58. The point where the shell struck the
target (see arrow and the positions on the tower).

now called Sde Yoav. This was the site of the Arab village of Iraq
Suidan. North of Route 35, there is a square building. This is
the site of the Iraq Suidan fortress. It is obvious that this police
station blocked Route 35, which was the road that connected
the southern part of the Negev to the northern part.

Picture 59. Kibbutz Negba (upper arrow) and Iraq Suidan (lower arrow)

C. The Involvement of HEMED in the Battles of the Fallujah Pocket

Fallujah was an Arab village located 30 kilometers northeast of Gaza City. The village and the neighboring village of Iraq al-Manshiyya formed part of the Fallujah Pocket, where four thousand Egyptian troops were besieged for four months by the newly established Israel Defense Forces. Several attacks were launched by Israeli troops to clear the pocket. The Alexandroni Brigade suffered heavy losses and HEMED was asked to help.

I joined the operation units and we camped at the abandoned Arab village of Hartia, near the entrance to the Fallujah Pocket. There we suffered from the bites of mosquitoes, fleas, and other bugs, but we could see that our Air Force was dropping our incendiary bombs on the Egyptian positions. Gideon Peleg (Pavlovic) recalls:

> We prepared incendiary bombs with solid fuel. They contained aluminum powder, gypsum, and magnesium. The weight of each bomb was one kilogram. And I saw that they set fires after being dropped from airplanes on the positions of the Fallujah Pocket (70).

Zvi Pelach, commander of the operation units, remembers:

> We used our M-2 canons placed on jeeps during an attack on Iraq al-Manshiyya. I do not know whether I caused any damage, but the noise was terrific. It was a good weapon, but sometimes our hands were injured during shootings (34).

CHAPTER 12:

OTHER HEMED UNITS

A. HEMED B

Avner Cohen described the activities of HEMED thus:

> In April 1948, Ben-Gurion asked Ehud Avriel[24] to find scientists who could save the lives of many citizens or, on the other hand, injure enemies. Ben-Gurion believed that we were the "chosen people," who should use scientific or technological means to protect our nation against enemy attacks. These arms could replace the lack of natural resources and the limited size of the Jewish population in our country (71, 72, translated from the Hebrew).

> Shimon Peres explained Ben-Gurion's idea as follows: Ben-Gurion believed that science could replace our lack of resources. It should be stressed that the development of chemical or biological weapons does not require unlimited funds, unlike nuclear weapons. The development of biological weapons requires well-trained personnel and laboratory space, both of which we had. The development of nuclear weapons is much more complicated and expensive. Therefore, we had to

---

24 Ehud Avriel was one of the figures behind the secret Haganah arms purchasing unit, Rekhesh, and later became an Israeli diplomat and politician and a member of the Knesset.

---

develop deterrent weapons. The development of nuclear weapons by Israeli scientists remained a mystery, even if some reports appeared in the press.

During World War I, Ben-Gurion was a law student at the University of Istanbul and was aware of the massacre of Armenians by Turkish troops. The Shoah, the Holocaust, in which many of his family members perished, convinced him that other nations would not rescue us in case of emergency.

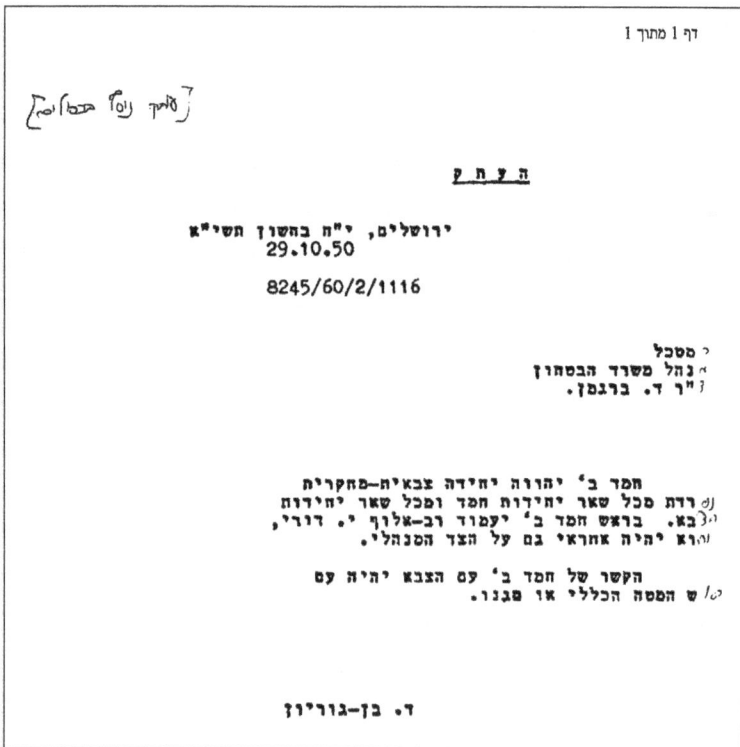

Picture 60. HEMED B was controlled by the chief of staff

The development of biological weapons by Israeli scientists was also kept confidential. According to Avner Cohen (72), Alexander Keynan suggested the formation of HEMED B and at the beginning of 1948, he asked Ben-Gurion and Yigael Yadin, the chief of staff of the Israel Defense Forces, to create a scientific unit that would develop and protect against biological weapons. Yadin and E.D. Bergmann recommended accepting this idea. On February 28, 1948, Keynan was ordered by Yadin to leave Jerusalem and form HEMED B, first in the Romano House in Tel Aviv and next in an abandoned building in Abu Kabir in Jaffa. From there, the unit moved to its final site in Ness Ziona, a city in central Israel. According to Ben-Gurion, the activities of HEMED B were under the command of the chief of staff and were top secret (Picture 60).

The activities of HEMED B were kept top secret. The only data published on HEMED B were those of Avner Cohen (71, 72) and Sara Leibovich-Dar (73). According to Sara Leibovich-Dar, Ephraim Katzir told her the following:

> I took part in the formation of HEMED B and we planned projects dealing with chemical and biological weapons. We considered the possibility that we would have to create tools to protect ourselves against enemy attacks. We have to know what is happening on the other side. We know that our neighbors are developing these weapons and our scientists should protect our country (73, translated from the Hebrew).

Indeed, we had information that the Egyptian army had mustard gas containers, left by the British when they left Egypt in 1973 (74, 75). Subsequently, Egyptian scientists established chemical industries (76), such as Abu Za'abal Company for Chemicals and Insecticides. The Egyptian army used chemical weapons in war in Yemen from 1967 to 1983 (77). It was not clear why the Egyptians used such deadly poisons in a relatively small war. Some experts claimed that Yemen was an experimental site where sophisticated tools were tested. Other experts claimed that mustard gas was used against rebels hiding in caves. Bombs containing mustard gas or phosgene caused the death of 1,500 rebels and more than 1,500 were injured (77).

It had been suspected that the Egyptian army had an arsenal of chemical weapons even before 1960. Therefore, there was good reason for HEMED to develop protective means. The first chemical attack by the Egyptian army was carried out in Yemen in June 1963. On January 5, 1967, Egyptian pilots bombed a village in southern Yemen with twenty-seven bombs containing a poisonous gas. This resulted in the killing of 270 civilians. On July 16, 1987, the village of Hajja was bombarded with sixty deadly bombs that killed between 425 and 520 inhabitants. In May 1967 the Egyptian army also used napalm (74).[25]

There were rumors that Israeli agents used chemical and biological weapons during the War of Independence (78, 79). On May 23, 1948, four Israeli soldiers were captured near Gaza City (80, 81). Ben-Gurion wrote in his diary on May 27, 1948, "Chief of Staff Yigael Yadin deciphered a cable sent from Gaza, saying that two Jews were arrested [and accused of] carrying malaria parasites. After three months the criminals were executed."

Yeruham Cohen, an Israeli intelligence officer, wrote in his book:

Lieutenant David Mizrachi and Lieutenant Ezra (Efgin) Horin crossed the Egyptian lines on May 12, 1948, near Gvar'am [a kibbutz in southern Israel] to retrieve information about the location of the Egyptian invading troops. They were supposed to stay behind enemy lines for about one week. We were first informed of the arrest of David Mizrachi and David Horin by a broadcast from Radio Cairo. From information published by the Egyptian press, we learned that two days after crossing the border, they were detected by local Arabs, who handed them over to Egyptian authorities. We learned that they were

---

25 Napalm, naphthenic and palmitic acids, is a thickening/gelling agent generally mixed with petroleum or a similar fuel for use in an incendiary device, primarily as an anti-personnel weapon.

tortured during a long interrogation and accused of planning to contaminate water sources.

> They insisted that they were innocent. But after serious torture they were forced to sign a confession. They were sentenced to death by a military court in Gaza. Three Egyptian soldiers claimed that they had arrested Mizrachi and Horin while the two were contaminating a well with poison (82, translated from the Hebrew).

We do not have any accurate information regarding whether Mizrachi and Horin were sent on a spying mission to obtain information concerning the movement of Egyptian forces, or whether they were sent to contaminate water sources.

In his book, Yeruham Cohen (82) included a copy of the "confession" of the arrested soldiers. This was written in Arabic with Hebrew. It is most likely that this "confession" was the result of cruel torture and suffering. Moreover, according to the report, the "criminals" were detected by local Arabs, while Egyptian soldiers claimed at the trial that they arrested the Israeli soldiers. It should, however, be stressed that dysentery bacteria caused diarrhea and discomfort and was not a lethal weapon.

The following description of the Israel Institute for Biological Research was provided by Thomas Gordon in his book:

> The [Israel] Institute for Biological Research is located twenty kilometers south of Tel Aviv. In its laboratories and workshops, various biological and chemical weapons are developed and produced. Chemists from the institute produced the poison that was used in an attempt to attack the head of Hamas's political bureau, Khaled Mashal.
>
> The institute's activities began in 1952 in a small underground bunker fortified with cement. Today, the insti-

tute has expanded to an area of forty square kilometers [this figure seems to be exaggerated and in fact the area does not exceed four square kilometers]. The originally planted trees were removed and instead a wall equipped with sensors was constructed. Armed guards patrol and protect the institute. Because of censorship, the site of the institute cannot be found on a map and the address and phone numbers are kept secret.

Most of the laboratories are underground and the scientists work with bottles containing "deadly agents," including poisons that cause food poisoning that could be lethal or cause physical damage.

Other scientists work in laboratories behind locked doors. There, they produce chemical warfare agents. Every month, all the scientists are subject to medical examinations. Even so, apparently six scientists have been infected and lost their lives. Military censorship did not permit the disclosure of the causes of their deaths (83).

In 1952, after the end of the War of Independence, the activities of HEMED as a military unit were changed and they became civilian-ruled bodies. HEMED B was similarly transferred to the prime minister's office, which funded its budget, and became a civilian institute for biological research. Alexander Keynan, the founder of the group, was appointed its first chairperson. He was succeeded by Robert Goldwasser (84).

According to an Internet source, the functions of the Israel Institute for Biological Research were defined as follows: "The research of the institute is focused on applied research, development, and production of tools in the field of chemistry, biology, ecology, and public health. Basic research related to these subjects is also carried out" (85). According to the same source, 320 scientists worked at the institute. Of them, 139 held doctoral degrees and 100 were well-trained technicians.

The institute was divided into three scientific sections: biology, chemistry, and environmental sciences.

In the 1950s, several similar centers were established in different countries. There, different chemical and biological weapons were developed for defensive and offensive purposes. Such centers existed in Porton in the United Kingdom and at Fort Detrick, home of the US Army Medical Research and Materiel Command (MRMC) and at the Walter Reed Army Institute of Research in Washington, DC.

Research at the Israel Institute for Biological Research was divided into two parts. The first was based on basic and applied sciences and was not secret. It was supported by foreign sources and its results could be freely published. Topics of research included Alzheimer's disease and methods for the cultivation of cells *in vitro*. The other part was strictly confidential and results of the studies could not be published. Some information leaked out after the arrest, in January 1963, of Prof. Avraham Marcus (Marek) Klingberg, who spied for the Soviet Union. Yet the extent of his crime, the nature of the secrets disclosed, and the damage caused to the State of Israel have never been disclosed.

A Dutch scientist, Karle Knap, reported (86) that microorganisms that caused plague, typhoid, and rabies were cultivated at the institute. Special attention was given to spreading disease by means of insects. Some information can also be obtained in published data. Thus, Jacob Mager published a paper on growing the pathogenic organism *Pasteurella tularensis* (87). More recently, it was revealed that the institute, in collaboration with the Israeli Medical Corps, developed a vaccine to protect against anthrax infection. The vaccine was injected into Israeli soldiers and caused harmful side effects.

The biological expertise of the institute was often applied to improve public health. According to Alexander Keynan (88), one of the important contributions of the Israel Institute for

Biological Research was the production of a vaccine to protect children against infection by polio viruses. During the 1950s, there was a polio outbreak and parents refrained from sending their children to schools or nurseries. Ben-Gurion asked Keynan to use the facilities of the institute to prepare a vaccine. At that time, the virologist Robert Goldwasser was working at the institute, but he did not have any experience in cultivating viruses in monkey kidney cells. Therefore, Natan Goldblum (Picture 61) was asked to accept responsibility for the development of an anti-polio vaccine.

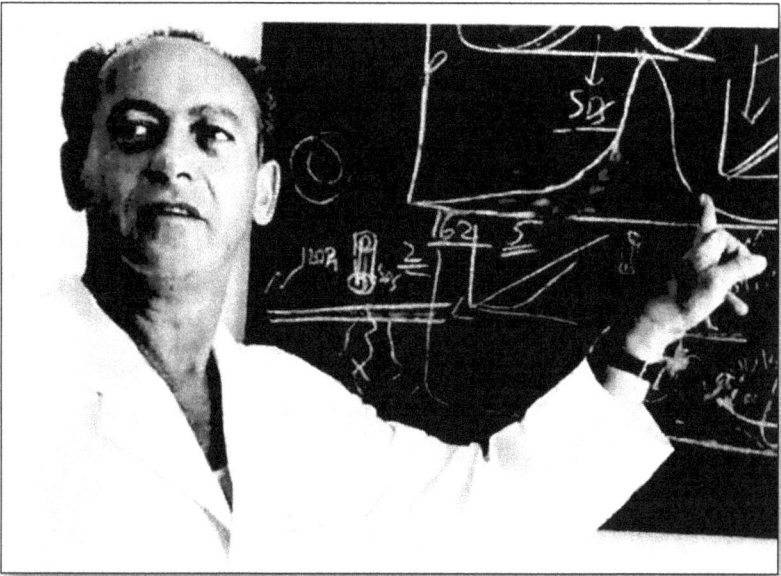

Picture 61. Natan Goldblum, who developed the vaccine against polio.

Goldblum was born in Poland in 1920. In 1951, he completed his PhD dissertation on malaria research. Thereafter, he worked at the laboratory of Joseph Melnick in Houston, Texas, where he specialized in growing viruses in cultured cells. Following his training in the United States, Goldblum served in the

Israeli Medical Corps (public health) at Tel Hashomer Medical Center. When he was asked by Alexander Keynan to move to the Israel Institute for Biological Research, he insisted that his colleague Abraham Marcus (Marek) Klingberg and his wife should move with him. As mentioned above, Klingberg was a Russian spy.

It was difficult to obtain monkeys from which kidney cells could be isolated. According to Keynan, he approached Mr. Mordechai Gazit, who was the Israeli consul in Burma, and asked him to buy Macacus rhesus monkeys. Gazit replied, "I see the monkeys jumping on the trees, but there is no one to catch them" (88).

Finally, monkeys were obtained and the anti-polio vaccine was prepared according to the method developed by Jonas Salk. Polio viruses were inactivated by treatment with formaldehyde and their immune activity (antigenicity) was tested. It was essential to inactivate all the viruses and that no viable viruses should survive. Similar attempts were made in the United States and in Denmark. Denmark was the first country to produce an active anti-polio vaccine and Israel was the second. The production of a vaccine in the United States was delayed, as some active viruses were detected in the vaccine. The Israeli vaccine was immediately used to protect children and indeed, immunized children did not suffer from polio and the outbreak was arrested. It thus appears that Goldblum and his group at the Israel Institute for Biological Research contributed much to the public health of the population of Israel and justified the institute's existence.

Prof. Van Der Huden, who was born in the Netherlands and survived the Holocaust, also worked at the Israel Institute for Biological Research and prepared vaccines to protect animals. This was another contribution of the institute to the improvement of farming and agriculture.

B. HEMED C

1. Touring the Negev Mountains

HEMED C was formed at the beginning of 1948, with the purpose of conducting geological studies to find out whether any important minerals could be detected in the southern part of Israel. Only later was attention shifted to exploring possibilities for finding minerals that could be used for nuclear research. The base of the unit was at the "Hill" near Rehovot, a place now called the Ayalon Institute, which was an ammunition factory, built illegally by the Haganah, where Sten guns and bullets were manufactured. Prof. Israel Dostrovsky of the Weizmann Institute was the founder of the unit and related the following:

> During the Mandate period, the British government sent geological expeditions to the Negev to explore the possibility of finding petrol and minerals. They explored the craters and other sites between the Dead Sea and the Red Sea (a seawater inlet of the Indian Ocean, lying between Africa and Asia). Jewish geologists were not permitted to visit those sites. After the end of the British Mandate, Israeli geologists could tour the Negev and the northern Sinai (89).

Picture 62 shows the team in the desert. This is an unusual picture, as Dostrovsky was rarely exposed to a photographer. Our team exploring the desert is shown in Picture 63.

Ben-Gurion instructed us to form a unit to explore those areas with the hope of finding oil and minerals. Ben-Gurion used to quote the Bible: "A land whose rocks are iron and out of whose hills you can dig copper." Israel Dostrovsky was appointed commander of the unit and assisted by the geologist Yaakov Ben-Tor from The Hebrew University and Akiva Furman from the Technion in Haifa.

Picture 62. The team in the desert (Dostrovsky is on the right; the second from the left is the geologist Akiva Furman).

Picture 63. Our team in the middle of nowhere.

Even before Dostrovsky's expeditions began, in the mid-1940 groups of students from The Hebrew University and members of the Palmach toured the mountains of the southern Negev to study the flora and fauna. But little attention was given to the geology of the Negev. A tour by the members of the Palmach was led by Haim Singer during July and August of 1944. Expeditions by students of botany and zoology were carried out from March 26 to April 4, 1945, and April 16 to

27, 1946. The first expedition included Jacob Wahrman (Picture 64), Daniel Zohary, Oded Becker-Arzi, Ze'ev Chavazelet, Pinchas Mishkov, Naftali Kaufmann, and Avraham Toren. The second expedition included Wahrman, Zohary, Kaufmann, Joseph Wiener, Jonah Levin, Uzi Narkis, Tuvia Kushnir, Avi Zakai, David Sulsberg, and Daniel Raz (90).

Picture 64. Jacob Wahrman touring the Negev

2. Expeditions of HEMED C

Yehezkel Ben-Ari was one of the guards at HEMED Base No. 1. Due to his devoted service he was promoted to commander of the guards at that base (36). When the operation unit of HEMED C was formed, he was asked to serve as the personal driver of Prof. Dostrovsky, commander of the unit. During his service, he met Aharon Donagi and Elhanan Diamant, professor of organic chemistry, who was the deputy director of the unit. Ben-Ari joined them in touring the hills of Hulekat in the northern Negev in an attempt to find oil. They also went south and explored the Small Crater (Picture 65).[26]

---

26 The Small Crater (*HaMakhtesh HaKatan* in Hebrew) is a geological erosion landform in Israel's Negev desert.

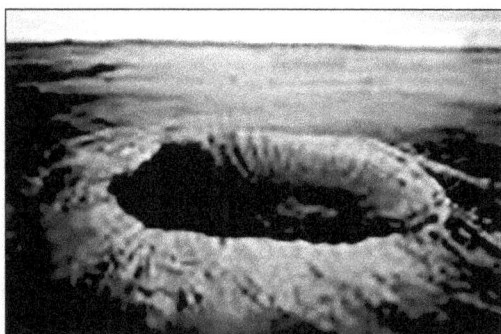

Picture 65. The Small Crater

Leah Macaresco (91) was a signal officer who served at the Palmach headquarters in Beer-Sheva. She was asked by her superiors whether she would be willing to join an expedition in the Negev Mountains and be the only woman among many men. They told her that she should not be afraid as the men were of special quality, being members of a secret unit called HEMED. She agreed and did not regret it as she married Yehezkel Ben-Ari, who was her associate in Hatrurim (Picture 66).

Picture 66. The camp in Hatrurim (courtesy of Yehezkel Ben-Ari)

3. I Join the First Expeditions

At the beginning of March 1949, I was sent to the officer training academy in the Dora Camp near Netanya. I was one of the few HEMED members sent to that course. Several days later, I was retrieved from the course and ordered to join a top secret mission. I returned to our base and was ordered to drive to Beer-Sheva, which had recently been conquered. There I reported to the Palmach command and was ordered to join an expedition by HEMED C. We were given a jeep, driven by Yehezkel Ben-Ari in the presence of Shimon Gatt and the signal officer, Leah Macaresco. We were instructed to proceed to the "Petrol Road" and to arrive at Mamsheet (Kurnub in Arabic).[27] There we would meet Dostrovsky and the geologists.

At that time, the Egyptian army still occupied that area and Eilat and Ein Gedi were not in our hands. So we crossed the lines and camped near Hatrurim (Picture 66). Since I was an expert in mining and demolition, I was responsible for placing trip flares around our encampment. I also used explosives to remove rocks that blocked the way of our vehicles. The geologists started their survey, collected rock specimens, and, after marking their positions, placed them in marked bags. Obviously, we did not wear uniforms, and we smoked English-made Players cigarettes and pretended to be foreigners. When asked by the local Bedouins about our activities, we responded that we were German engineers who were testing the possibility of constructing a railway through these mountains. We added that if we achieved our goal, they would all become rich because of commerce and tourism. They agreed with us and even helped us to carry minerals to our tents. As a reward, they received some cigarettes. The Bedouins saw the geologist Ben-Tor jumping from one hill to the other and called him *Abu Hunfus* (grasshopper).

---

27 Mamsheet was a Nabataean city and an important station on the Incense Road.

We were divided into small groups and communicated with each other and with Macaresco by walkie-talkie. Macaresco had direct contact with HEMED's headquarter at Base No. 1, so we could be evacuated by air in case of emergency. During one of the surveys, one of the Bedouins approached me and said in Arabic, *"Ana aref shu hada. Hada wireless."* ("I know what this is. This is a wireless."). I asked him how he knew. He answered that he was a soldier in the Arab Legion of the Kingdom of Jordan and that he was trained to use this device. Again, we had to repeat our story of being German engineers and the problem was solved.

We suffered from a shortage of food. Water could be collected from ponds filled with rain water, but we did not have food. The Air Force supplied us with concentrated food designed by Dr. Bernstein. This concentrated food consisted of a paste of fruit extracts that was given to Israeli pilots who could use it in emergencies if their plane crashed or was abandoned over enemy territory. This "food" caused constipation and we did not want to taste anything for the next several days.

We completed our survey, collected our belongings, and prepared ourselves to return to "our country." Suddenly we heard a loud noise and the sound of rolling rocks. Jacob Wahrman, who had previously hiked in the Negev, recognized the noise and shouted, "This is a flood; we have to get out immediately." We packed our tents and belongings, put them in our jeeps, and rushed up to the mountains (Picture 67). One truck was stuck in the water and we had to wait several hours until the water level declined. When we approached the vehicle, we could not start it and we had to feed the engine with fuel through a plastic pipe. Finally, we reached Kibbutz Nevatim, wet and exhausted. Picture 68 shows Shimon Gatt in the front of our tent after returning from the "expedition". He is unshaven, looks tired, and is wearing a British army coat.

Picture 67. Flood in the desert

The collected minerals were brought to the analytical laboratory on the "Hill" and the results of the analytical data were disclosed on May 10, 1949. Based on the findings that phosphate deposits may contain uranium, Ben-Gurion decided at the end of 1949 to send promising young Israeli physicists to scientific institutes abroad to study nuclear physics. After the end of their training they returned to Weizmann Institute

Picture 68. Shimon Gatt in front of our tent after returning from the expedition.

in Rehovot, which paid the amount of 500, 000 Israeli liras to the government of Israel.

On February 4, 1952, the following message was sent from the prime minister's office to E.D. Bergmann (Picture 69):

> HEMED C (the Atomic Energy Commission). Mr. Levinson met with us and stressed the need to start the use of atomic energy for constructive purposes. McDaniel also agreed with this approach. This sounds reasonable. The budget indicated in my list is only for starting the activities. It is most likely that we will succeed in our mission. [translated from the Hebrew]

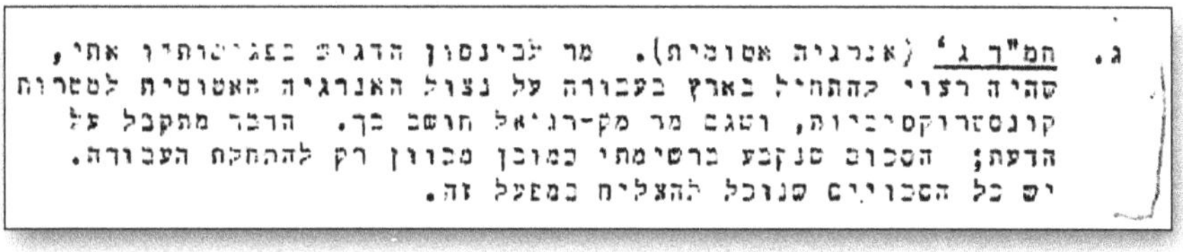

ג. חמ"ד ג' (אנרגיה אטומית). מר לבינסון הדגיש בשיחותיו אתי,
שהיה רצוי להתחיל בארץ בעבודה על נצול האנרגיה האטומית למטרות
קונסטרוקטיביות, וגם מר מק-דניאל חושב כך. הדבר מתקבל על
הדעת; הסכום שנקבע ברשימתי כמובן מכוון רק להתחלת העבודה.
יש כל הסכויים שנוכל להצליח במפעל זה.

Picture 69. A message to E. D. Bergmann changing the name of HEMED C to the Atomic Energy Commission.

4. Results of the Expedition

We do not have the results of the chemical analyses conducted at the "Hill," but some information that indicated that the phosphate layers contained small amounts of uranium leaked. Avner Cohen mentioned in his book (92) a letter sent on May 10, 1954, by E.D. Bergmann to Prof. Gunnar Randers from the Norwegian Institute for Atomic Energy: "We have just finished the development of a procedure for extracting uranium from phosphate rocks. It appears that the process is economically feasible even if the concentration of uranium in the rocks is low. We are now considering the construction of a plant that could produce five to ten tons of uranium annually." According to Cohen (93), "Before the Six-Day War (1967), Israel had the capability of nuclear weapons." Myer Feldman, who was an aide to President John F. Kennedy, disclosed that before the crisis of the Six-Day War, the government of the United States was aware that Israel had two atomic bombs. It was very likely that the nuclear material needed for the production of the bombs originated from uranium isolated from phosphate deposits. Feldman reported the following:

From January 17 to January 18, 1964, an American scientific delegation visited the Negev Nuclear Research Center in Dimona [Picture 70] to explore the existence of "remarkable plants." They were especially interested in determining the fate of the waste fuel of the reactor. They were told that the first fuel was supplied by the French Atomic Energy Commission and the waste was returned to them. In addition to the uranium supplied by France, Israel had at least nineteen tons of natural uranium from its own sources (94).

Declassified KH-4 CORONA November 11 1968

Picture 70. The completed complex of the Negev Nuclear Research Center in Dimona as seen by the American Corona satellite on November 11, 1968.

In 1954, an agreement on the commercial use of the process for producing uranium from phosphate deposits was signed between the French government and the Israeli Ministry of Defense (94). Tom Segev stated in a broadcasted interview that Shimon Peres objected to starting a war before the Six-Day War (95). He suggested that a threat to use nuclear weapons would deter enemies. It thus appears that Shimon Peres knew that we had nuclear weapons before June 1967. Munya Mardor, founder of Rafael (the Armament Development Authority) wrote in his diary on May 28, 1967, "When I came to the assembly hall, I found [name deleted] inspecting a group of technicians who were active in assembling a secret weapon that they had designed and produced before the outbreak of the war. Members of the team were aware of the value of the weapon, which was ready for operation."

CHAPTER 13:

····•••••••◦◦●———•••◦•••———●◦•◦••••••••·····

SCIENTIFIC RESEARCH AT HEMED BASE NO. 1

In June 1948, soon after independence was declared, we were sworn in under the command of Ephraim Katzir. We all received the tag of the unit (Picture 71). My number was 14422.

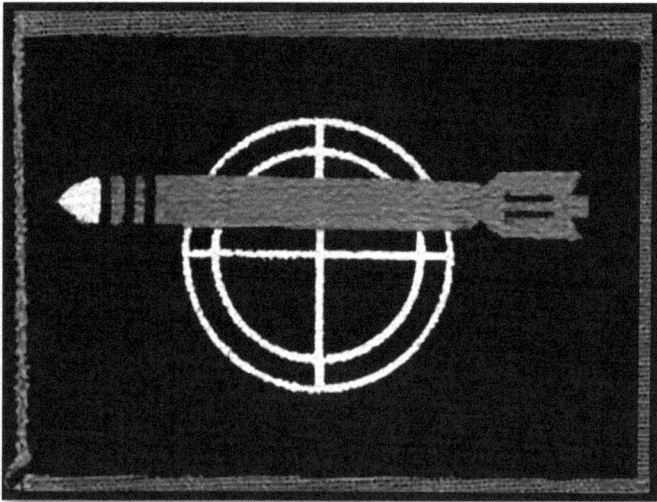

Picture 71. The HEMED Science Corps tag

A. The HEMED Maneuver in Herzliya

Ben-Gurion conceived the idea of establishing a Science Corps and was interested in its activities. It was therefore decided to invite him to a maneuver in which we would demonstrate our achievements. This event took place on June 20, 1948, on the sands near the shore of the Mediterranean near Herzliya in a place called Sidna Ali (Picture 72). It is important to note that this maneuver was performed only two months after activities at HEMED Base No.1 had begun in Tel Haim. The program was as follows:

SCIENCE CORPS (HEMED): MANEUVER NO. 4 (JUNE 20, 1948)

1. Anti-tank weapons
   A. Molotov cocktail
      A glass bottle containing fuel and wrapped with chemicals. Ignited by breaking the bottle. Effective range: 10–30 meters.
   B. Small flame thrower
      An incendiary device designed to project a long, controllable stream of fire. Can be carried on the back and fired five times, three seconds each. Ignited by firing bullets. Effective range: 45 meters.
   C. Long-range flame thrower
      Can be installed on a vehicle and has an electronic ignition. Effective range: 80-100 meters.
   D. PIAT (Projector Infantry Anti-Tank) weapon (see Picture 36)
      Has a maximal range of 340 meters and a hollow charge explosive. It can penetrate 80–100-millimeter-thick iron or 30-millimeter-thick concrete. Effective range: 100–120 meters.

E. Three-inch anti-tank cannon

Can be mounted on a vehicle, placed on a position, or carried by hand. Shells with hollow-charged explosives can penetrate 80-millimeter-thick iron. Effective range: 400 meters.

F. Recoilless gun

A lightweight weapon that fires a heavier projectile from a recoilless gun. Still in development stage. Effective range: 500 meters.

G. Six-inch heavy mortar

Has a 45-kilogram shell and can be fired to a range of 3,500 meters and transported on wheels.

Picture 72. The maneuver at Herzliya. Standing from right to left: Lola Schweiger, Alon Feldman-Radler-Talmi, Aharon Katzir, Abraham Berman, Natan Spiegler Sharon, Atida Littauer, Josepha Friedman, Y. Friedman, Ernst Fischer, Gideon Greenberg, Mark, Aviv Peleg (Feldbrovsky), Hoenig, Yoske Feintuch. Second row from right to left: not identified, Zvi Pelach, Emmanuel Goldschlag, Zvi Appenschlag, Sarah Perel, Israel Miller, not identified. Third row from right to left: fourth from the right wearing a hat is Yair Klivanski, then Israel Pelach, Zvi Racheli, Ephraim Harnick, Shlomo Burstein, Gideon Peleg (Pavlovic). On the far left: the author with a bomb. Front row from right to left: guards Bezalel Tidhar and Shulik Sapir.

H. Air-borne incendiary bomb
   Each 3-kilogram bomb produces concentrated fire.

I. Flare air bombs.
   These are thrown from airplanes to illuminate at night.

J. Smoke bombs

Visit at the Exhibition

In his diary entry from June 20, 1948, Ben-Gurion wrote that he attended the arms tests in Herzliya (Picture 73), noting: "We have PIAT weapons, with a range of 100–200 meters that penetrate 80–100 millimeters of iron and have a range of 400 meters." He was impressed by the demonstrations and the explanations provided by Aharon Katzir, and he promised to continue his support.

Picture 73. Ben-Gurion inspecting the maneuver. Near him is Uri Littauer (in shorts), commander of the chemists, and Aharon Donagi is to his left. Shlomo Gur is in the back.

It had been expected that the invading enemy armies would be supplied with tanks and/or armored vehicles. Therefore, it was essential to produce primitive anti-armor weapons. Attention was focused on the production of Molotov cocktails. In fact, the development of Molotov cocktails and the production of shells for PIAT were started by Taas before 1948, but the design and the production were improved by scientists from HEMED.

Flame throwers, which were developed by HEMED, were not used widely during the War of Independence. Attempts to use flame throwers from vehicles failed, as they did not reach the effective range of 120 meters. However, it has been claimed (96) that during the battles in Ramat Rachel (May 25, 1948), flame throwers were used. Amos Chorev also recalled that flame throwers were used in Jerusalem. In the battles on the road between Gaza and Rafiach on January 3, 1949, flame throwers were used (96).

Anti-tank cannons: Two-inch diameter cannons were used in the battlefield. According to Gideon Yekutieli (60), Uri Habersheim planned to fire hollow-charged shells from a two-inch cannon in order to hit Syrian tanks in the Upper Galilee (near Yesud Hama'ala). This activity was cancelled by the ceasefire on June 10, 1948. Asher Asher reported that he used these cannons to stop Jordanian troops near Beit Nabala (not far from Ben Gurion Airport). Similar cannons were used in the Fallujah Pocket. Zvi Pelach, who was the commander of an operation, placed these guns on jeeps and was very satisfied with their performance.

Recoilless guns: The development of these guns was completed in Haifa only several years later.

Six-inch heavy mortars: These mortars were designed by Jenka Ratner in January 1948. They were perfected by Aharon Strikovsky of Taas. This mortar was successfully used in the battle on Iraq Suidan on November 9, 1948.

B. The Meeting of the Incendiary Group

The Incendiary Group was the largest and the most active group in HEMED. The first meeting was held on September 22, 1948, and addressed both theory and application. The theoretical part included two sections:

1. incendiary weapons
2. pyrotechnical weapons, used for marking and illumination

The section on incendiary weapons included lectures on the following:

- Fuels as military incendiary weapons (Gideon Pavlovic)
- Thermites[28] as incendiary weapons (Uriel Bachrach)
- Use of fuel in incendiary bombs, shells, and grenades (Aviv Feldbrovsky)
- Molotov cocktails (Torecki)
- Flame throwers: control of fuel (Nathan Sharon)
- Flares and photo flash bombs
- The use of these weapons was also demonstrated in field tests.

C. The Development of New Weapons

Shlomo Burstein, a chemistry student, searched scientific literature for information that we could use to develop new weapons. At the beginning of March of 1948, he brought me a

---

28 Thermite: Oxidation of a metal, such as aluminum or magnesium, by an oxygen-rich component. It is reported that the reaction may reach a temperature of approximately 3,000°C.

journal published at the end of World War II by the German army. The title of the journal was something like "Information on Explosives and Propellants." This journal was found by American intelligence services and found its way to Burstein. Since I could read German, I found two interesting chapters, one dealing with thermites and the other describing tear gas bullets.

1. Thermites

Thermite reactions are based on the oxidation of a metal such as aluminum or magnesium by an oxygen-rich component. This reaction, which generates heat, is used commercially for welding metals, but could also be used for military purposes. It appears that Aharon Katchalsky attempted to develop a "thermite bomb" in the early 1940s. In 1947, he repeated his experiments together with Abraham Berman, who was injured by an unexpected explosion. Apparently, Amos Chorev succeeded in preparing a thermite-based incendiary bomb.

Incendiary bombs were widely used in World War II. The German city of Dresden was completely burned out by allied bombing. Various types of incendiary bombs were used at the time:

A. "Light" bombs containing magnesium, weighing 2 kilograms each, were dropped from planes in clusters.
B. Solid fuel bombs, which could contain napalm. These could reach a weight of 250 kilograms.

At the end of World War II, German scientists reported that $CaSO_4$ (gypsum, plaster of Paris) could replace expensive oxygen-rich nitrates or chlorates. We did not have any information regarding whether such inexpensive thermite bombs were used by the German Luftwaffe. I was attracted by the idea of designing gypsum-thermite bombs, since gypsum deposits were found in the Jordan Valley and were readily available.

THERMITE BOMBS

Magnesium and aluminum powders were required for the production of thermite bombs. Aluminum powder was commercially used for the production of paints and could therefore be obtained from hardware stores. On the other hand, magnesium powder or strips were not readily available. They could be used for photography, but their price was high. We found out that airplane wheels were rich in magnesium and decided that this would be the source of the needed metal. Therefore, whenever an enemy plane was shot down, we collected its wheels and cut them into small fragments. One day, a new recruit appeared and said, "I am Ephraim Levkovich from the Hakoach Sports Club of Vienna, Austria." At that time, I was not familiar with this sports club, but I gave Levkovich a 10-kilogram hammer and asked him to break the wheels. Several years later, Ephraim Levkovich changed his name, and Dr. Ephraim Lahav became the scientific attaché at the Israeli Embassy in Washington, DC, and subsequently represented The Hebrew University in Germany.

We soon realized that hammering the wheels was both difficult and time consuming. Therefore we decided to use explosives to shatter them instead. We covered the wheels with sand bags, put the explosives in place, and recovered the fragments. I used an empty area near the "Brown House" at HEMED Base No.1 and did not realize that an aerial for broadcasting was constructed there. In one of the explosions, the aerial was hit and the broadcast of the declaration of independence was almost disrupted.

2. The Use of Tear Gas Bullets

Prior to the establishment of the State, Taas and Agan Chemicals produced tear gas hand grenades. These weapons, which contained chloroacetophenone (CHAP) could be used only for short-range operations, and could not be thrown from a distance exceeding 40 meters. Tear gas bullets had two advantages. They could be fired at distant targets and they were precise. I discussed the idea of using them with Uri Littauer, my commander, and decided to remove the bullet from the cartridge, drill a hole into it, and fill it with molten CHAP. The bullet was then sealed with glue or lead and placed back into the cartridge. We prepared such bullets and marked them with yellow paint. We demonstrated that the yellow bullets could be fired into a window at a distance of several hundred meters. When the bullet hit the wall, the CHAP was released and tear gas spread throughout the building. Yair Klivanski was appointed to produce these bullets in large quantities and Uri Littauer took some of them to the northern front and fired them into enemy positions. Yehuda Venezia brought some bullets to the Galilee and gave them to a sniper, who succeeded in repelling enemy soldiers from a fortified position.

I was impressed by these preliminary tests and suggested that tear gas bullets could also be used as an anti-tank weapon. On the night of June 29–30, 1948, British soldiers left Palestine via Haifa. Several of them defected and brought with them two Cromwell tanks (97). Based on my suggestion, one of these tanks (Picture 74) was brought to Beit Guvrin. In the presence of Yitzhak Sadeh, I fired several tear gas bullets from a Bren machine gun. The bullets hit the tank and CHAP was smeared on its outer armor. The tank had an air circulation system, which sucked fresh air into the tank. This system pumped CHAP into the tank and the crew had to escape. I do not know whether this idea has ever been applied practically.

Picture 74. A Cromwell tank

3. Report on HEMED Accomplishments

Four months after the HEMED maneuver at Herzliya, enough information had been collected and it was time to summarize the results of the research conducted at HEMED Base No. 1. This was a classified report and written by the section heads. Some of them had not yet mastered the Hebrew language. It was also evident that some of them were not trained to write scientific reports. Therefore, some reports were too detailed, while others were too brief. In any case, one has to appreciate their work, considering the fact that many of them were young scientists, students, or engineers who had never been exposed to the problems of chemical warfare. The achievements of these scientists were based on close collaboration with mechanical workshops and the purchasing department. Without their vital assistance, research and development would have been doomed.

On October 23, 1948, a classified report was published. Its goals were:

1. To draw the attention of military personnel to newly developed weapons.

2. To draw the attention of military personnel to the fact that a new research and development department had been established. This department could accept requests to develop new weapons, or, alternatively, propose the use of newly developed arms.

CHAPTER 14:

REVIEW OF THE SCIENTIFIC RESEARCH CONDUCTED AT HEMED BASE NO. 1

A classified report written on October 23, 1948, describes the scientific research carried out at HEMED Base No. 1 (98) as follows:

Classified:

Until now, the scientific research carried out at Base No. 1 has not been summarized. In this report we review the achievements of the different disciplines. This is of great interest, as some of the results have been accepted by the Army and used in practical applications.

    a. Propellants
    b. Explosives
    c. Thermites
    d. Incendiary weapons, based on liquid fuel used for bombs, shells, and hand grenades
    e. White phosphorus
    f. Tear gas
    g. Smoke
    h. Signals from planes or guns

i. Parachute flares

j. Photo flash bombs

k. Delay devices

l. Crackers

Comments: This report was written six months after the establishment of HEMED Base No. 1. During this short period, impressive results were obtained, despite the limited resources available and the lack of previous experience by the young scientists. The high level of motivation and the devotion of the scientists led to unexpected results.

A. Propellants

This chapter is clearly written. Some excerpts from it appear below.

The research focused on the extrusion of cordite (Picture 35), a family of smokeless propellants. It was soon discovered that the rate of burning could be varied by changing the surface area of the cordite. Narrow sticks were used in small arms and were relatively fast-burning, while thicker sticks would burn more slowly and were used for longer barrels, such as those used in artillery and naval guns. We used acetone to permit extrusion.

The use of acetone to soften cordite was studied by Chaim Weizmann at the University of Manchester. During World War I, he produced acetone by fermenting corn with *Clostridium acetobutylicum*. This was an important contribution to the war effort of the allied forces.

B. Explosives

This chapter deals with the production of explosives. Special attention was given to penta-erythritol-tetranitrate (PTEN).

This explosive was first produced in the 1930s by Hugo Hei-mann, from the Chemical Engineering Department at the Tech-nion. In 1939, it was prepared in the Jafora orange juice factory in Rehovot. In 1943 (during World War II), the pharmacologist Felix Bergmann (E.D. Bergmann's brother) was in charge of preparing ten tons of PTEN in a workshop in the Beit Herut settlement. He was assisted by "the doctor," Asher Schweiger (Shamgar). Benyamin Shapiro also improved the methods of PTEN production during his work at the Sieff Institute in Re-hovot in 1948.

PTEN was also used as an explosive in torpedoes, self-propelled warheads launched above or below the water surface, propelled underwater toward a target (used by the Israeli Navy) and in hollow-charged shells. Six to seven scientists worked in this group, which was one of the largest at HEMED Base No. 1.

Zelina Shatil (Picture 75) was a member of this group. She was born in Poland and survived the Holocaust. She succeeded in immigrating to Palestine and began her studies in the Chemi-cal Engineering Department at the Technion. When the War of Independence broke out, she joined the Carmeli Brigade, where her husband also served. Unfortunately, he was killed in action during battle in Haifa. Zelina Shatil could not stay in Haifa after the death of her husband, so in May of 1948, she moved to Tel Aviv and joined HEMED. Her first task was to prepare Molotov cocktails, which were sent to Kibbutz Degania in the Jordan Valley to protect it from the attacks by Syrian tanks. One of the "cocktails" exploded during preparation and Sha-til's sister-in-law was wounded. Later Shatil was transferred to another group working with explosives that was headed by Dr. Ephraim Lahav, who attempted to improve the detonation of TNT by pressing the explosive into shells using a special press (99). This was a very dangerous task, and Shatil asked to be transferred to another group, where the work was not so dan-gerous, so she had to find a candidate who was willing to re-place her. She approached Zvi Appenschlag, who served on the base in Jerusalem, and asked him to move to Tel Aviv. Appenschlag agreed, since he wanted to be close to his mother, who lived there. Shatil trained him and asked him to take part in a field test in Kibbutz Haogen, where a powerful hydraulic press could be used. Shatil, Appenschlag, and a chemical engineer called Meir came to the kibbutz and Shatil left them to go for a swim in the sea. In the meantime, the team started to use the press, an explosion occurred, Appenschlag was killed, Zimmerman (a member of the kibbutz) lost his eyes, and Meir's hands were seriously injured. Shatil moved to another group, headed by Zvi Tzur, where she could use her training as a chemical engineer (Picture 76).

Picture 75. Zelina Shatil

Another member of the group was Yitzhak Modai (Picture 77), an Israeli businessman and politician, who later became a minister in the government (99). At the end of the war, studies at the Technion started again. Shatil left HEMED and completed her studies in chemical engineering, after which she began to work at the Israel Standards Institute in Tel Aviv.

Picture 76.
The chemical plant

Picture 77. The chemical team

C. Thermites

This chapter focuses on incendiary weapons. In early 1946, the Haganah command decided to attack the Mandatory immigration office in Jerusalem, destroy it, and burn the documents connected with illegal immigrants. Aharon Katchalsky found a document describing the preparation of a thermite incendiary bomb. This consisted of a metal such as magnesium or aluminum and an oxidized metal. These bombs generate heat that can melt iron (100). Some bombs were prepared and the archives in Jerusalem (and perhaps also in Tel Aviv) were destroyed (101,102).

Picture 78. The author and Josepha Friedman preparing thermite bombs.

In his workshops at The Hebrew University in Jerusalem, Elik Sochazewer prepared "bagels" containing incendiary materials. These were supposed to damage electricity and telephone poles.

Unfortunately, the British Police found these "bagels" but could not explain their function.

A classified report from December 12, 1948 stateds:

> The group that dealt with incendiary weapons and pyrotechnical devices started its activities approximately six months ago. The number of scientists in the group was relatively limited (four to six). Nevertheless, impressive results were obtained and some of the products were produced by the [Military] Industry. We prepared thermite bombs of a weight of 3 kilograms each [see Picture 78] and also hand grenades. The flames produced by these thermites generated heat of 1,000–2,000°C and could melt iron (103).

At HEMED Base No. 1, there was a water tower that supplied water to nearby buildings. On May 27, 1948, I climbed up the tower with a bomb, which I planned to throw down. When I pulled the safety pin, an explosion occurred and a fire was started. My hand and leg were burned and I had trouble descending the tower. I was rushed to a military hospital. My wounds were treated and I received morphine to relieve my pain. I was told that I would have to remain in the hospital for one week, but after four days (on June 1, 1948), I felt better and decided to return to my unit. I found my overall, which was stained with blood, and escaped from the hospital. When I reached the bus station, I did not have money to pay the fare. Luckily one of the passengers saw a poor wounded soldier and paid for my ticket. Picture 78 shows how I prepared new thermite bombs with a bandage on my left hand. I was wearing a new overall and I was assisted by Josepha Friedman, who mixed the ignition materials in a drum prepared in our workshop.

Shaike Yarkoni (husband of the renowned Israeli singer Yaffa Yarkoni) was a liaison officer between HEMED and the

Israeli Air Force. He reserved a Dakota aircraft from the Air Force base at Sde Dov, north of Tel Aviv, to perform an aerial test. We flew over the sand hills above the beach and dropped bombs from different altitudes. We soon found out that if the bombs were dropped from altitudes higher than 2,000 feet, the bombs disintegrated because the metal envelopes were not thick enough. Yarkoni asked, "What does the bomb contain?" I answered that they contained gypsum. He responded, "Take cement instead of gypsum. Cement is stronger." Obviously, his recommendation was not accepted. In addition to the 3-kilogram aerial bombs, we attempted to prepare mortar shells filled with thermite. The main purpose was to use them at night. Two different types, tracer shells and regular shells, were planned. In the first type, ignition started soon after firing, when the shell was still in the air, so that its route was visible. In the second type, ignition was started when the shell hit the ground and the target could be recognized (103).

D. Incendiary Weapons

Liquid fuel

This section deals with the use of liquid fuels that contain mazut (fuel oil) or similar fuels, which are less expensive than gasoline. The main problem was the high ignition temperature. In order to solve this problem, we used a thermite starter, which, after its ignition, generated enough heat to start the fire. We used this idea to load Davidka shells with liquid fuel.

Napalm, a solid fuel, was first developed by L. Fieser in the United States. It contains aluminum salts, naphthenic, and palmitic acids. This weapon was used successfully by the allied forces during World War II. Napalm was prepared in large quantities in the Yitzhar factory, which produced soap. Eliyahu Caspi, Yirmiyahu Jaffe, and Nathan Sharon were in charge of production, while research and development were conducted at the Israel Standards Institute in Tel Aviv by Nathan Sharon, Shaya Gallili, and Eliyahu Caspi. (For more information on this matter, please see the report on flame throwers.)

E. White Phosphorus

This section addresses the military use of white phosphorus. During World War II, hand grenades filled with white phosphorus were used as anti-personnel and incendiary weapons.

The group studying the potential of this weapon encountered the following difficulties:

1. Dealing with this weapon was dangerous and indeed one of the researchers (Gideon Pavlovic) was wounded while filling grenades with this chemical.
2. White phosphorus is unstable.
3. White phosphorus is expensive.

Field studies did not justify the use of this weapon. Cheaper incendiary weapons were available and the anti-personnel effect remained doubtful. Therefore white phosphorus was not used during the War of Independence.

F. Tear Gas

This section deals with tear gas, one of the most impressive tools applied in the battlefield. As mentioned above, tear gas was produced as early as 1944 by scientists from The Hebrew University. In 1945, a plant called Agan Chemicals was established in the Motza settlement, west of Jerusalem. In 1946, Zvi Tzur and his associates began to prepare tear gas required by the Haganah. Bromine was needed for production and Abraham Berman risked his life and brought 30 kilograms of bromine from Potash Industries at the Dead Sea. By February 2, 1948, Agan Chemicals prepared 100 kilograms of tear gas containing chloroacetophenone (CHAP). This material was incorporated into rifle bullets and used in practical applications. It should be noted that tear gas is used as a conventional, legitimate weapon by police and other security forces.

A classified report from December 12, 1948, states:

> It has been suggested that we entrap CHAP in rifle bullets. Field studies have demonstrated that if the bullet hits a solid target such as metal or concrete, it disintegrates and the tear gas is spread into the surrounding area. Several bullets can inactivate people in a confined space, such as a room or vehicle. More than 10,000 bullets containing CHAP were prepared at HEMED Base No. 1. More bullets are now being prepared by Taas using improved technology (103, translated from the Hebrew).

Ben-Gurion was aware of the development of weapons containing tear gas. He called it "Samson" and in his diary he wrote on January 14, 1948:

> Within six weeks our industry will start the production of a new weapon that can be used for the following purposes:
>
> Mortar shells for a distance of 1,500 meters and small ones for a range of 100 meters.
>
> Hand grenades: range of 10 meters.
>
> Jenka Ratner started to prepare mortar shells containing "Samson" on February 5, 1948.
>
> One to two scientists are involved in this project (104).

G. Parachute Flares

Projects that focused on signals (H.) and delayed explosives (K.) did not receive much attention. The parachute flare project was supported by the Israeli Air Force, which planned to use the flares for night attacks by plane. Because of the embargo, these flares could not be obtained from other sources and therefore the request was urgent.

Shimon Gatt (Picture 79) and Yehudit Birk prepared the flares. They contained gypsum for ignition and were attached to parachutes (which luckily did not fail and opened after being dropped from the planes). Yehudit Birk said that she was flying with Shaike Yarkoni, the liaison officer between HEMED and the Air Force, in a Piper aircraft (Picture 80) (105). She was warned by Yarkoni that if the parachute did not open, he would shoot her. Luckily, Birk remained alive, as the parachute did not fail. Subsequently flares equipped with small parachutes were also prepared for 52-millimeter mortar shells.

Picture 79.
Shimon Gatt in uniform

Picture 80. Piper aircraft

H. Photo Flash Bombs

This section deals with the development of flash bombs, which were requested by the Israeli Air Force. Initial attempts were based on information retrieved from other countries. A report from September 19, 1948, states:

In peace time, flash lights are commonly used for photography in rooms and therefore only a limited light source is required. In times of war, flash bombs are dropped from airplanes. For this operation, high intensity light is required and many of the devices are quite heavy. The German Luftwaffe used 50-kilogram flash bombs and the British Air Force used 15-kilogram bombs (106, translated from the Hebrew).

Picture 81. A photo flash bomb

We developed 7.6-kilogram flash bombs. Each bomb had a parachute and after adding magnesium strips, light emission reached 19 million candles (Picture 81). Small bombs were designed to be fired from two-inch mortars. These bombs contained a parachute that was activated after shooting.

I. Crackers

This section deals with the developments of crackers, the effect of which should resemble that obtained by shooting a six-pound shell from a cannon. We received a number of thunder crackers produced by foreign countries and analyzed their contents. Crackers were prepared based on chemical analyses (106) and gave satisfactory results (Picture 82). Similar crackers were later used by police forces to disperse demonstrations.

Picture 82. A thunder cracker explosion

On April 2, 1948, Abraham Berman suggested that HEMED appoint heads of departments. This suggestion was never implemented. However, it appears that I acted as the head of the incendiary and pyrotechnical group, as I wrote classified report no. 103 and no. 106. Research on delayed fuses did not receive much attention and was soon discontinued.

CHAPTER 15:

·······•••••••——••••••••——•••••••••·······

ATTEMPTS TO DEVELOP NEW WEAPONS

A. The Development of a New PIAT (Projector Infantry Anti-Tank) Weapon

During the 1936–1939 Arab revolt in Palestine, Haganah commanders believed that attacks were the best way to defend settlements and that a brave soldier penetrating enemy positions could contribute more than attacks with tanks and/or cannons. This concept was changed in 1947, with the knowledge that our enemies would use artillery and tanks for their attacks. Haganah commanders decided that anti-tank weapons should be developed to neutralize tanks and armored vehicles (27).

PIAT weapons could fulfill these functions. They weigh approximately 15 kilograms, with a barrel one meter long and a range of about 100 meters (see Picture 36.) Israeli soldiers in the British forces were trained to use this weapon during World War II. One these was General Israel Tal (who later developed the Israeli Merkava tank). He and his associates knew that PIAT shells contained a hollow-charged explosive that could pierce the armor of a tank. At the end of 1947, Ben-Gurion called a special meeting and said, "In view of the expected invasion of Arab military forces, we have to produce anti-tank weapons. PIAT is a good option." He asked Chaim Slavin (head of Taas) what he thought. Slavin answered, "If you think that the development of this weapon is essential, I will try to do it, but it will take eight months." Jenka Ratner shouted, "Slavin is a perfectionist. If the production of PIAT is so important, I will do it in a shorter time." Slavin stood up and shouted, "Jenka is a liar. If necessary, I will do it within six months, and Jenka cannot do it within two years." Shlomo Gur asked Slavin, "What will happen if in the meantime the Jordanian legion invades us with its armored cars?" Slavin answered, "I will take my children and we will go to the sea." Finally, Jenka Ratner was asked to develop the PIAT (27).

After many negotiations, Ratner received a small amount of TNT from his rival Slavin, and he prepared a shell with a hollow charge. On November 13, 1947, he invited all the experts to a demonstration at Kibbutz Dalia on Mount Carmel. He prepared steel plates 25 millimeters thick. All those present were surprised to see that the charge drilled a hole through the steel plates. Slavin, who was present at the demonstration, was not impressed and said, "Look and see what this charlatan [Ratner] did. Do you really believe that the hollow charge did it? We all know that the charlatan drilled a hole ahead of time!"

On December 11, 1947, Ben-Gurion wrote in his diary, "Experiments with the PIAT weapon were carried out in Kibbutz Dalia. We hope that by the end of December the experiments can be concluded" (107). The first experiments with hollow-charged explosives were carried out in 1946 by Amos Chorev and Abraham Berman in Kibbutz Beit HaArava near the Dead Sea. Amos Chorev told the following story:

In 1946, I was the commander of Company H of the Palmach in the Jerusalem District. At that time, I became interested in anti-tank weapons. I found some information in the *London Illustrated News*, where the anti-tank weapon PIAT had been described. In that magazine, the structure of the PIAT was provided. I spoke with Abraham Berman and suggested that we develop a PIAT. I approached my father, Elik Sochazewer, and Mr. Levinson, head of the physics laboratories at The Hebrew University, and requested their help. Mr. Spitzer was a metal smith and had his workshop on Jaffa Street in Jerusalem. He prepared the envelope for the hollow-charged shell. We melted TNT and poured it into the shell… We also inserted a concave liner and started the field experiments in Kibbutz Beit HaArava. We constructed the shell, but we did not have any information concerning the PIAT launcher. At that time, my company was stationed in Kibbutz Ma'aleh Hachamisha, west of Jerusalem. Near our kibbutz there was a Palestinian village, Abu Gosh. I knew some smugglers who lived in that village and asked them to steal a PIAT launcher from a British Army camp. They did it, but I had to pay them 70 pounds, given to me by my father. I passed the launcher on to Jenka Ratner, who reproduced it with the help of Taas in Tel Aviv (12, translated from the Hebrew).

After the PIAT launcher was given to Jenka Ratner, Simcha Blass, an Israeli water engineer, reported:

The director, A (director of Taas), told me that he had received an order from the chief of staff to produce some kind of weapon. Only after three weeks did he reveal that the order was to copy a British anti-tank weapon called PIAT. He told me that he had in his possession a sample of the weapon and asked me if we could produce 150 copies. I answered that if it was urgent we could do it, but we would need six months. Then I asked him if he could hand the weapon over to me. We drove to his home and he took out a big bag and gave it to me.

Our first task was to separate the different parts of the weapon, to draw them and to clarify their composition. After doing this, we had to find workshops that could copy the parts. This was not easy. A director of a workshop that produced iron bed stands could produce the 80-millimeter diameter barrels. He took his time and delayed production so that his sons would not be drafted to serve in the army. Some others demanded high prices. On the other hand, there were others who volunteered to do it without being paid (26). To copy the spring of the PIAT we needed a steel wire one-quarter inch in diameter. Such a wire could not be found anywhere in the country. Sasha Goldberg, from the Technion, was a British citizen and he succeeded in purchasing 2,000 kilograms of steel wires. Unfortunately, they were 6 millimeters in diameter instead of a quarter of an inch. Therefore, several springs had to be incorporated into each barrel. This was done by Techno Springs in Tel Aviv (27) (108, translated from the Hebrew).

The production of PIAT shells was not easy. One shell was smuggled out of South Africa and Jenka Ratner separated the different components and studied their composition. The drawings of the parts were given to Simcha Blass, who started to manufacture them. The explosive in the shells had to be TNT, which was needed for the hollow charge. Contaminated TNT could be smuggled from Italy, where it was retrieved from old World War II ammunition (such as artillery shells). This contaminated explosive had to be purified before casting it in PIAT shells. TNT was available only in the Tel Aviv district. Jerusalem, which was isolated, had to obtain it from the crude material smuggled out of Italy. Elik Sochazewer volunteered to carry out the dangerous purification process. He borrowed a 150-liter pot from the Cooperative Restaurant in Jerusalem, filled it with water, and inserted a smaller 100-liter pot into the water. He put the crude explosive into the small pot and the larger pot with water was placed on a primus burner (Picture 83).

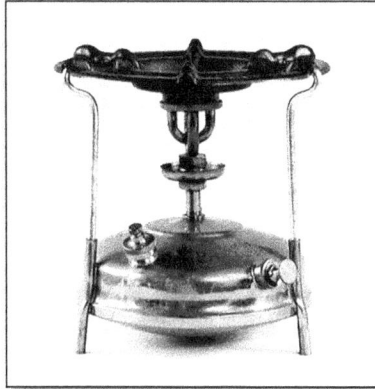

Picture 83. A primus burner

When the TNT in the small pot reached a temperature of 81°C, it melted and the contaminants floated up. This was an extremely dangerous process. Sochazewer risked his life, but provided Jerusalem with explosives needed for the production of PIAT shells.

With the first samples of the shells, field studies began. A water tower in an orchard near Tel Aviv was the target. The shell hit the water tower and penetrated its cement walls. In addition, holes were pierced through 60-millimeter thick steel plates. Based on the success of the field studies, the Haganah ordered 48,000 shells to be manufactured by Taas (27).

The PIAT weapon was used successfully during the War of Independence. One fighter in Kibbutz Negba fired seven PIAT shells against attacking Egyptian tanks. Six of them hit the enemy tanks, stopping them in their tracks, and the kibbutz was saved. The importance of the PIAT was also demonstrated during the battle at the Nabi Yusha fortress[29] (Picture 84). This fortress blocked the road leading from Tiberias to the northern part of the country. Only PIAT shells could penetrate its solid walls (26). During the War of Independence, PIAT was the only significant anti-tank weapon (with the exception of primitive Molotov cocktails).

From 1948 to 1949, Taas produced 750 PIAT launchers and 17,000 shells (28). This is a good example of the outstanding initiative and devotion of Jenka Ratner, who, together with other HEMED scientists, copied an existing weapon and introduced it to the IDF.

Picture 84. The Nabi Yusha fortress in the Upper Galilee

B. The Development of Flame Throwers

Many Haganah commanders believed that flame throwers would be the weapon that would neutralize fortified positions. Sasha Goldberg, a chemist and engineer, emigrated from

---

29 Nabi Yusha was a fortress that commanded the main road to the Upper Galilee and the routes to the Jewish settlements of Ramot Naftali and Manara. Forty-eight Palmach fighters lost their lives attacking Nabi Yusha.

England to Palestine in 1940, bringing with him information about flame throwers. In 1942, he returned to England and worked as a civilian for the war office. He isolated magnesium from sea water, developed large flame throwers designed for fighting in jungles, and offered his assistance (27). After the end of the war, he was sent to India to reconstruct a plant for the production of planes. On the way to India, he stopped in Palestine, and during one of his visits he met with Ben-Gurion. In 1947, he decided to settle in Palestine. There he continued his work on flame throwers, which he had started in England (109). He was assisted by Dr. Torecki from the Technion.

Ben-Gurion recommended forming a Department of Scientific Production and Coordination, to be headed by Goldberg, with Ora Herzog as its secretary. Goldberg started the research on flame throwers and their production. He encountered difficulties in cooperating with Chaim Slavin and Jenka Ratner, but despite these problems, he succeeded in producing forty small flame throwers (with a range of 40 meters) and several large ones with a range of 160 meters. Amos Chorev received six flame throwers, which he transferred to Jerusalem, where they were given to the Moriah Battalion (109).

In the Unites States, different types of flame throwers were designed. Others were produced in the United Kingdom and in the Soviet Union. Jenka Ratner, assisted by architects Yaakov Rechter and Haim Murro, suggested designing an original Israeli flame thrower that would have an advantage over known products. Many members of the department did not agree with him, and Levi Eshkol, the Israeli minister of finance, asked the opinion of engineer Yitzhak Vilenchuk, head of the Emergency Military Industry Committee. He decided that the British flame thrower should be selected. Simcha Blass manufactured flame throwers for short and long ranges and also designed a special revolver with an electric ignition (27).

We had no information concerning fuel for the flame throwers, except that it consisted of napalm. We received samples from different sources and these were sent to the Israel Standards Institute in Tel Aviv for analysis. Yirmiyahu Jaffe, director of the chemical laboratory at the institute, reported at the first meeting of the incendiary group on September 22, 1948:

> Even before the formation of HEMED, in January 1948, Haganah commanders decided that flame throwers should be developed. They approached the Israel Standards Institute, knowing that skilled scientists who had modern equipment worked there. When we studied the composition of the fuel, we came across a publication by L. Fieser, an American scientist who described the composition of napalm.
>
> On January 19, 1948, Eliyahu Caspi joined Leon Bloch, Mr. Rabinovich, and Ms. Wolfsberg and formed a team to develop fuel for the flame throwers. When HEMED was established, the team was reinforced by Nathan Sharon, Eliyahu Teomim, and Yeshayahu Gallili. Sasha Goldberg brought from England the information that aluminum stearate should be dissolved in benzene. We were asked to prepare several hundred kilograms of this fuel within several days, so that field studies could be started. On January 27, 1948, we prepared the first batch of 40 kilograms, and on February 2 we tested the fuel using small and large flame throwers. The mechanical parts of the flame throwers were prepared by Haim Murro and architect Moshe Zarchi. The ignition pistol was prepared by Arieh Damiel (Schweiger). [translated from the Hebrew]

Damiel recalls:

> I was born in Tel Aviv. After graduating high school, I joined Kibbutz Hamadia, in the Beit She'an Valley. In 1944, I left the kibbutz and studied chemistry at The Hebrew University of Jerusalem. At the end of 1947,

Abraham Berman asked me to join a secret unit that was supposed to prepare bromoacetone for tear gas. The synthesis of this compound was carried out in Aharon Katchalsky's laboratory on Mount Scopus.

After November 1947, I was recruited to join a Hish battalion and was sent to Kibbutz Beit HaArava to be trained as a platoon commander. Next, I was sent to the Old City of Jerusalem. When HEMED was formed, I was transferred from the Old City and was asked to take part in the development of flame throwers. Hayuta Fogel and Sarah Perel belonged to my group.

We started to prepare ignition bullets for the flame throwers. If I am not mistaken, Prof. Ernst Alexander of the Department of Physics started to prepare fuel for the flame throwers [Picture 85]. This was before the activities of Nathan Sharon and Yeshayahu Gallili at the Israel Standards Institute in Tel Aviv began. I moved from Jerusalem to Tel Aviv and developed an ignition pistol with a burning time of three seconds. This pistol was subsequently manufactured by Taas (51, translated from the Hebrew).

Picture 85. The large flame thrower in operation (courtesy of N. Sharon).

Attempts to use large flame throwers for conquering the fortresses of Latrun and Iraq Suidan failed. The half-trucks we used were unable to reach the targets and remained beyond the effective range of the flame throwers. According to Yehuda Ben-Zur, Israeli half-trucks (Picture 86) were equipped with flame throwers when Regiment 9 of the Negev Brigade of the Palmach attacked the Egyptian positions in Auja al-Hafir during Operation Horev (December 22, 1948, to January 8, 1949). Apparently, this weapon was not used during that operation (32). On the other hand, Egyptian soldiers used flame throwers when Israeli troops defended Hill No. 69 in the Negev on December 22, 1948.

Picture 86. A flame thrower on an Israeli half-truck during Operation Horev.

According to Netanel Lorch:

> Four Egyptian half-trucks equipped with flame throwers attacked Israeli troops who defended the hill. The uniforms of some of the defenders were charred by the fire, but the rest counterattacked, threw hand grenades, shouted, climbed on the attacking vehicles, and turned the fire from the flame throwers back against the attacking Egyptians (110).

HEMED and Taas continued the research and development of flame throwers. Picture 87 shows a well-dressed Israeli soldier (wearing a tie!) carrying a portable flame thrower. In Picture 88, Sasha Goldberg is pouring fuel into a small flame thrower. In conclusion, considerable efforts, manpower, and resources were invested in developing and manufacturing flame throwers. Unfortunately, this weapon was not successfully used during the War of Independence.

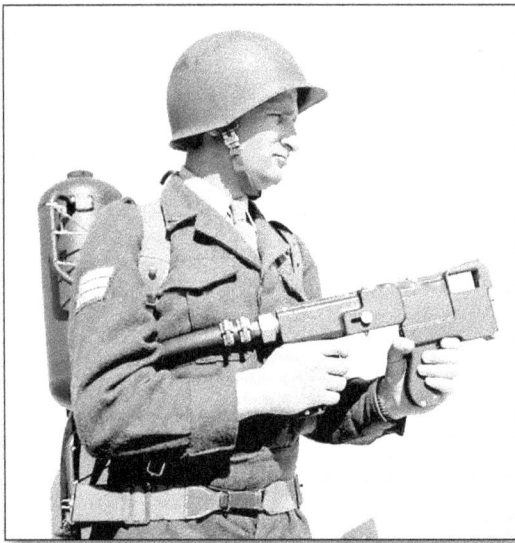

Picture 87. An Israeli sergeant carrying a flame thrower.

Picture 88. Sasha Goldberg filling a flame thrower with fuel.

C. The Development of Rockets

The development and production of flame throwers and PIAT launchers were mainly based on copying items used by different foreign armies. As rockets could not be purchased from foreign countries, it was decided that Israeli scientists and engineers would design and produce them. Obviously, this was a very ambitious task that required time and resources. Therefore the development and production of original rockets took time and was completed only after the end of the War of Independence, when HEMED no longer existed and had been replaced in 1949 by Rafael. Ephraim Katzir summarized the sequence of these events in his lecture at the Israel Academy of Science and Humanities:

There was a time when we thought that the production of rockets and missiles would be important for our security. One day, I heard that a Jewish scientist lived in Paris and that he knew something about rockets. I asked for more information and I was told that his name was Moshe Feldenkrais and that he was born on May 6, 1904, in Slavuta, in the present-day Ukrainian Republic. In 1930, Feldenkrais moved to Paris and enrolled in an engineering college, the École Spéciale des Travaux Publics de Paris. He graduated in 1933 with specialties in mechanical and electrical engineering. He left Paris during World War II and worked for the British Navy in the United Kingdom. After the war, he returned to Paris.

After receiving the information about Feldenkrais, I went to Ben-Gurion and told him that we had to bring this French scientist to our country. Ben-Gurion answered: "Bring him!" I knew that if Ben-Gurion said "Bring him," it would be my problem and I would not receive his support. So I went to Paris and met Feldenkrais at a dinner organized by Baroness Batsheva de Rothschild. I convinced Feldenkrais to come to Israel and to help us in developing rockets.

After Feldenkrais arrived in Israel, I asked David Wofsi to find him a laboratory at the Weizmann Institute in Rehovot. One month later, Wofsi contacted me and said, "Feldenkrais has been working in his laboratory for one month. Let us go and see the results of his research." So we went to his laboratory and on the bench we saw something that looked like a wine goblet covered with a glass resembling a mushroom. I asked Feldenkrais, "Will this creature fly?" Wofsi answered, "It will never fly, but it will be good for tourism. We can show our guests that in addition to rockets we can create some art at our institute."

Wofsi refused to have him anymore and I did not know what to do with him. So I asked Feldenkrais, now we know that you are an expert in designing rockets, what else do you know? He said, "I can stand on my head." I told this to my brother Aharon, who told this to Ben-Gurion, who started to stand on his head [Picture 89]. This was an important contribution of HEMED to Ben-Gurion's head (62).

STEF WERTHEIMER

Stef Wertheimer was born in 1926 in Oppenheim (the Black Forest) in Germany (111). His family left Germany and settled in Tel Aviv and Wertheimer studied at Tel Nordau High School. After Wertheimer's graduation, his father recommended that he learn a profession and sent him to an optical store on Allenby Street in Tel Aviv.

Picture 89. Ben-Gurion standing on his head.

Picture 90. Stef Wertheimer

After a year and a half, he knew the secrets of optics. Next, he specialized in repairing cameras. After completing this training, he joined the British Army, where he repaired optical instruments. In 1944, he was released from the British Army and joined the Palmach. At first, he worked at a mechanical workshop in a kibbutz and then he was ordered to join an illegal training course for pilots in Kibbutz Naan (Picture 90). One day, Aharon Donagi approached him and asked whether he could construct a rocket according to the drawings made by physicists Amos De Shalit and Gideon Yekutieli. He agreed and together with one of his comrades, prepared a rocket (Picture 91). In the presence of high commanders of the Palmach, the rocket was fired. Unfortunately, it landed near a group of Indian soldiers in the British Army camp of Sarafend. They shouted, "*Allah Akbar.*" British policemen and soldiers searched for the source of the shooting. The training camp in Kibbutz Naan was dismantled and the pilot course was transferred to another kibbutz in the north. A Russian immigrant named Grisha claimed that he was an expert in constructing rockets. It turned out that the only thing he knew was how to drink vodka. So this story also ended (112).

Wertheimer continued to develop new rockets. One of them is displayed in Park 65 in Kfar Vradim in the Galilee. During the War of Independence, Wertheimer constructed a small rocket in the mechanical workshop of Kibbutz Kfar Giladi. He named it the "Flea" (111). He explains: "I started to develop the Flea during March and April 1948 according to the drawings made by Jenka Ratner (Picture 92). I demonstrated the activity of that weapon near the police station of Rosh Pina in the presence of Yigal Allon. This weapon was called the *Parosh* ("Flea") because it was not as heavy as the Davidka and could be carried by soldiers." As mentioned above, the *Parosh* was used during the War of Independence in the battles of Iraq Suidan.

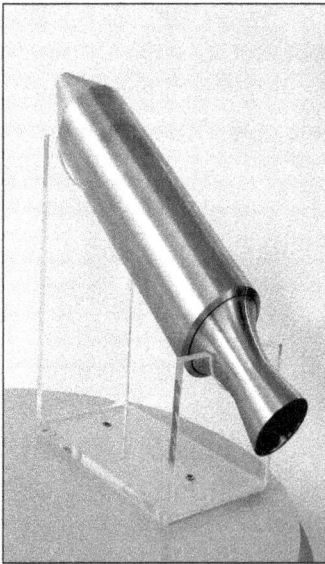

Picture 91. The rocket that was constructed by Stef Wertheimer.

The development of more sophisticated rockets continued at the HEMED bases in Haifa and Curdani. Special attention was given to the development of naval rockets. This was done by Uzi Sharon, who was encouraged by Yedidia Shamir (head of Rafael) and by Jenka Ratner. Uzi Sharon joined the Palmach in 1946 and started his training as a pilot. He had to leave the course due to illness and was transferred to Kibbutz Givat Hashloshsa, where he produced explosives that were sent to Gush Etzion (113).

Picture 92. The Parosh, designed and manufactured by Stef Wertheimer (displayed in a museum in Kfar Giladi).

In early 1947, he was approached by a Palmach commander named Dov Zayces, who asked him whether he knew anything about torpedoes, self-propelled weapons with explosive warheads. Sharon answered that all he knew about torpedoes was based on what he had seen in movies and read in books. Zayces gave him five pounds sterling and instructed him to travel to the port in Haifa and meet Yohai Ben-Nun, the commander of the Palyam. Ben-Nun asked him to design a remote-controlled boat to damage British destroyers that were preventing the arrival of "illegal" Jewish immigrants. He also told him that the work should be done in Jerusalem under the supervision of Elik Sochazewer at the physics laboratories at The Hebrew University. Sharon completed the design of such a boat and decided to test it in the fish ponds of Kibbutz Maoz Haim. He navigated the boat with an electrical wire and the experiment succeeded. When he repeated the experiment in the open sea near Caesarea, waves shocked the boat and it sank. Yohai Ben-Nun was not discouraged and asked him whether he could design a "remote-controlled naval missile" with a range of 1,800 meters. Sharon agreed and set out to design a missile, which he called the "Shark." After two months of intensive work he produced two "Sharks" with the help of Jenka Ratner, who prepared the fuses in the HEMED laboratories.

In July 1947, the ship *Exodus* attempted to approach the shores of Palestine with 4,500 "illegal" Jewish Holocaust survivors on board (Picture 93). It was intercepted by a British destroyer and, following a struggle, the immigrants were arrested and sent to a prison near Haifa.

Picture 93. The Exodus as it was towed into the port of Haifa, after its interception by a British destroyer.

The Haganah commanders and the leaders of the Jewish Agency decided that British destroyers should be damaged to prevent similar interceptions in the future. Sharon was asked to prepare his "Sharks." "Sharks" were loaded onto a fishing boat and an attack was planned for the following night in the presence of leaders and commanders of the Haganah. Suddenly, a currier arrived on a motorcycle with a message from Ben-Gurion, who ordered them to cancel the operation in order not to provoke the British government on the eve of their departure from Palestine (113).

From 1947 to 1948, Uzi Sharon improved his "Sharks" with the help of HEMED scientists Yedidia Shamir and Jonathan Maas. The next step (1948–1953) was devoted to the design and production of "Seals" and G-11 torpedo boats, which were used by the Israeli Navy. The Shafrir air-to-air missile (Picture 94), which was developed in the 1950s, was the result of the design of the "Seals."

Moshe (Moja) Epstein contributed much to the development of rockets (59). He was born in Tel Aviv in 1925 and after graduating from high school joined the Palestinian Coast Guard. At the end of his service, in 1944, he enrolled at the Technion and studied mechanical engineering.

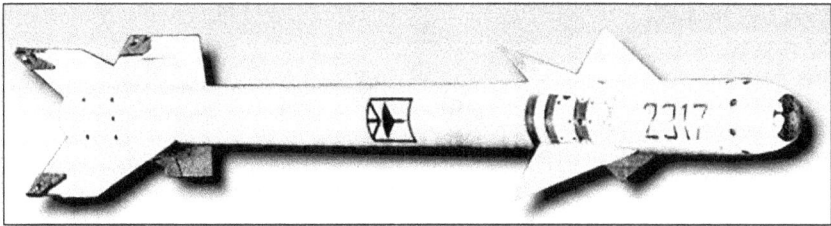

Picture 94. The Shafrir air-to-air missile was developed by Rafael and used by the Israeli Air Force.

During his studies he met Moshe Ish-Shalom (a Haganah commander), who took Epstein and Chanoch Peruz to Jenka Ratner's office. Epstein started to develop new weapons. At the beginning of 1948, he joined a group of physicists, headed by Amos De Shalit, who were attempting to develop a recoilless gun, a lightweight weapon that fires a heavier projectile (*"tolar"* in Hebrew). The research was conducted at HEMED Base No. 1, in the presence of Meir Birk, who studied the velocity of the fired shells. Moshe Epstein explained:

> We were trying to develop a recoilless gun, but we could not find any information. We did not have raw materials and had to start from zero. We used a water pipe as a barrel and fastened it with a wire. Later, we found some pipes that the British had left in Helez, where they conducted surveys for the detection of oil. In 1949, we first demonstrated the use of the newly developed weapon and hit a target at a distance of 800 meters [Picture 95]. The gun was placed on a stand that was used as a stand for a Browning machine gun (114).

Picture 95. A 55-millimeter diameter recoilless gun (courtesy of Moshe Epstein).

Despite the success in firing missiles from the recoilless gun, the Israeli Army did not show much interest in producing this weapon. Therefore Moshe Epstein requested a meeting with the chief of staff to ask for his support. The General asked, "How do you know that you are able to produce this weapon? Have you ever done it?" Epstein answered, "How did you know that you were able to act as a chief of staff? Had you ever done it (59)?" He received the support he needed. Subsequently, Epstein and his team developed a 75-millimeter diameter recoilless gun (Picture 96).

Picture 96. A 75-millimeter diameter recoilless gun developed by Rafael. From left to right: Denver Alexander and Moshe Epstein in the HEMED uniform (courtesy of Moshe Epstein).

Ephraim Katzir described how, during one of the maneuvers, the newly developed rockets were tested. Ezer Weizman[30] stood in the front of the target. When he was asked what he was doing there, he replied, "This is the safest place; the rocket will never hit the target." They removed him and indeed the rocket did hit the target (62).

---

30 Ezer Weizman was the sixth commander of the Israeli Air Force.

Epstein shared another example of the lack of confidence of the Israeli leaders concerning the development of new weapons:

Jonathan Maas planned to develop a new rocket, guided by radar... We met with Ben-Gurion who stated, "We are a poor country, we cannot afford radar." So we had to use primitive optical devices. Only ten years later, the Israeli Aircraft Industries introduced radars to guide Gabriel missiles. So we can see that with time impossible problems can be resolved (115).

Motti Hod, who followed Ezer Weizman as commander of the Israeli Air Force, claimed that he did not need missiles. He could solve the problem using guns. Only after some of his planes were downed by enemy missiles did he agree that missiles were necessary.

When research and development of the Angel ("*Malach*" in Hebrew) began, resources were limited. Therefore the first attempts to produce missiles were based on construction with wood rather than metal frames. Carpenters at the Technion were very helpful in preparing these wooden rockets. Moja Epstein constructed engines that resembled the V-1 and V-2 rockets developed by Wernher von Braun. He used liquid propellants. Other countries, for example the United States and the Soviet Union, tried to copy this system and produced the Atlas and Scud rockets, respectively.

In 1950, Epstein was sent to England to buy steel for the production of canons. He had false documents and was called "Avni" and received a budget of three pounds sterling. He was assisted by Arie Sarig, head of the purchasing department, and Feldenkrais, who was in London at that time. Before returning to Israel in 1952, Epstein visited the Imperial War Museum and found copies of German V-1 missiles (59).

D. The Development of Liquid-propelled Missiles by the IDF, 1952–1958

Moshe Epstein was appointed by the IDF's Research and Development Department to lead a research group assigned to develop liquid-propelled missiles. He was assisted by a subcommittee headed by Eliyahu Zahavi, who was charged with copying the engine of the German V-1 missiles, and another subcommittee headed by Yeshayahu Jarnicki, who was supposed to produce liquid-based missiles similar to V-2 rockets. At the beginning, members of the groups looked for printed information in magazines and books. A book on rockets published by the American expert George P. Sutton served as an important source of information. A dramatic change occurred in 1953 when Epstein visited the workshops of Oerlikon, one of the world's leading high-tech industrial groups, in Switzerland.

Another group was supposed to arrive at the same time as Epstein's group was visiting the workshop. That group had paid a substantial amount of money so that their members could visit and inspect the department that dealt with ground-to-air missiles. Somehow Epstein's group was mistaken for the paying group, so they received detailed information concerning the newly developed rockets. As a result, the Angel and the Lightning (*"Bazak"* in Hebrew) replaced the primitive Luz missile. Later, the Gabriel missile was produced. Based on these activities, Moshe Epstein was awarded Israel Security Prizes in 1984, 1960, and 1997 (Picture 97).

In 1960, three Israel Security Prizes were awarded; two of them were granted to scientists who worked at Rafael, Moshe Epstein, Jonathan Maas, and Anselm Yaron, who received the first prize together for developing guided missiles. The second group from Rafael was headed by Dov Katz and Ruth Kort, who received the prize for developing synthetic propellants. The third prize was awarded to electronic engineers who did not belong to Rafael.

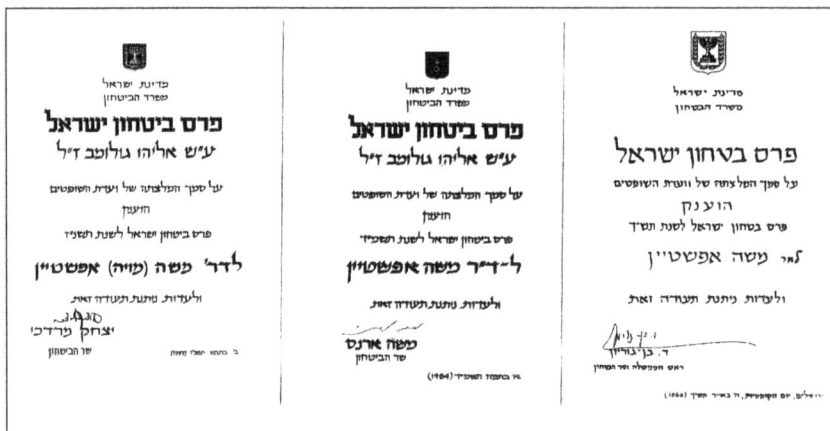

Picture 97. The three Israel Security Prizes awarded to Moshe Epstein.

The following scientists were awarded Israel Security Prizes:

Alexander Rosen (Lt. Colonel) was born in 1925 and during the Mandate served as a technician in the Palestine Broadcasting Service. Following the establishment of the State of Israel, he joined the Signal Corps.

Zvi Vardiel (Captain) was born in 1927 and studied electronics at ORT High School. During the War of Independence he served in the Palmach and finally joined the Signal Corps.

Anselm Yaron was born in 1918, graduated as a mechanical engineer in Italy, and worked in the petrol industry. He came to Palestine on the *Exodus* and joined the Ministry of Defense as a researcher.

Ze'ev Miller was born in 1923 and graduated from the Technion in Haifa as an electrical engineer.

Dov Katz was born in 1923 and began his studies in 1944 as a chemical engineer at the Technion in Haifa. He joined HEMED during the War of Independence. Later, he spent some time in Italy, specializing in the research and development of plasticware. Subsequently he returned to Israel and worked for the Ministry of Defense. He received his doctorate from The Hebrew University.

Ruth Kort graduated from The Hebrew University and developed synthetic propellants. She also received her doctorate from The Hebrew University.

Picture 98. Moshe Epstein and his team receiving the Israel Security Prize. Seated from right to left: Moshe Epstein, Ruth Kort, David Ben-Gurion, Dov Katz, and Anselm Yaron. Standing from right to left: Zvi Vardiel, Ze'ev Miller, Shimon Peres, Alexander Rosen, and Jonathan Maas (117).

Jonathan Maas was born in 1911. He graduated from the Technion in Haifa and served in the Jewish Brigade during World War II. He joined the Ministry of Defense as a researcher.

Since 1958, scientists from Rafael have received thirty-six prizes (Picture 98), more than any other research group in the country (59).

CHAPTER 16:

························ SCIENTISTS WHO PLAYED A
SIGNIFICANT ROLE IN ESTABLISHING HEMED

A. Aharon Katzir (Katchalsky), HEMED Founder

Aharon Katchalsky (Picture 99) was respected by Ben-Gurion, who asked him to find young scientists to form a scientific unit under Haganah command. This activity commenced on February 1, 1948, and the unit was named the Onn Company (Katchalsky's code name). Katchalsky was also present at field tests conducted on June 20, 1948, near Herzliya. Katchalsky served as commander of HEMED until the return of his brother Ephraim from the United States.

Picture 99. Aharon Katzir (Katchalsky), the first commander of HEMED.

Katchalsky was born in 1913 in the city of Lodz in Poland. In 1922, he and his family moved from Poland and settled in Jerusalem. Katchalsky attended elementary school and high school in Jerusalem and in 1930 began to study life sciences, biophysics, and polymers at The Hebrew University. In 1936, he published a book called *The Children of the Sun*, which classifies the butterflies of the Holy Land, together with Prof. Shimon Bodenheimer.

In 1939, he earned a PhD in chemistry with honors and was appointed senior assistant in the Department of Organic Chemistry at The Hebrew University. At this time, he broadened his knowledge in physics and mathematics in order to advance his research in life sciences. Katchalsky's laboratory was used by members of the Haganah, among them Amos Chorev, who used the facilities to produce explosives. Together with Prof. Yeshayahu Leibowitz and Dr. Moshe Brill, he published a book titled *Scientific Discoveries and Warfare* in 1943. In 1948, Chaim Weizmann invited Katchalsky to act as the chairman of the newly established Department of Polymer Research at the Weizmann Institute in Rehovot. He served in this capacity until he was murdered by a Japanese terrorist at Ben Gurion Airport on May 30, 1972. Under Katchalsky's guidance, the newly formed department developed rapidly and specialized in studying the functions of macro-molecules in biological processes, with an emphasis on clarifying the function of muscles. In 1965, he published a book on biochemistry that was used as a standard textbook in many universities around the world. His brilliant lectures attracted the attention of many students and young scientists. He published a fascinating book, *The Basis of Scientific Revolutions*, which included transcriptions of his discussions with Ben-Gurion.

Katchalsky conceived the idea of forming the Israel Academy of Science and Humanities and served as its first president. In light of his important scientific publications, he was awarded honorary degrees from various universities and served as president of the International Union of Theoretical and

Applied Biophysics. He was one of the few Israeli scientists elected as a member of the American National Academy of Sciences. His students continued and promoted the research and teaching of biophysics.

B. Ephraim Katzir (Katchalsky)

Ephraim Katzir (Picture 100) was born in 1916 in Kiev (Ukraine). When he was six years old, his family immigrated to Palestine and settled in Tel Aviv. Several years later they moved to Jerusalem and his father opened a textile shop on David Yelin Street. Ephraim Katzir graduated from the Hebrew High School in Rehavia, and in 1932 he began his studies at The Hebrew University.

At the age of sixteen, he joined the Haganah and four years later he graduated from a Haganah platoon commanding course. Subsequently, he completed the officer training course in Yavne'el, a settlement in northern Palestine. This was the most advanced course offered by the Haganah. He was appointed commander of a company in Jerusalem and Yitzhak Navon and Alex Keynan were his adjutants. The second company commander was David Amiran, and his wife Ruth was the secretary of the regiment, which included both companies (35).

Picture 100.
Ephraim Katzir (Katchalsky)

After completing his studies at The Hebrew University, he was appointed assistant in the Department of Theoretical Organic Chemistry by Prof. Max Frankel. There he specialized in research on polymers. During his work at The Hebrew University, he and his brother Aharon used the facilities and produced tear gas for the Haganah. Benny Marshak, a senior officer in the Palmach, asked him to study the properties of explosives. He became an expert in the field.

In 1947, Katzir was invited by Prof. Max Herman of the Brooklyn Polytechnic Institute in the United States to join his institute as a visiting scientist. During his work at the institute, he continued his activities for the Haganah and, together with Teddy Kollek he purchased military equipment.

At the beginning of May 1948, Katzir was asked to return to Israel. He, Teddy Kollek, and Colonel David Marcus[31] were stuck in Paris on their way to Palestine. Only on May 14 were they able to fly to Tel Aviv. This was the first plane to land in the newly formed State. After his arrival in Israel, Katzir was appointed commander of HEMED, replacing his brother Aharon. After the war, he returned to The Hebrew University as a professor and in 1949 was invited by the Weizmann Institute in Rehovot to serve as chairman of the newly opened Department of Biophysics.

In 1951, he was appointed visiting scientist at the Department of Physical Chemistry, headed by John Edsall, at Harvard University. There he specialized in protein research. His research in biophysics was highly appreciated by scientific communities around the world.

Katzir continued his activities for the security of the State of Israel and in the 1960s he became a scientific advisor of the Israeli Department of Defense. In 1973, Katzir was appointed

31 David Daniel "Mickey" Marcus (February 22, 1901–June 10, 1948) was a United States Army colonel who assisted Israel during the War of Independence in 1948.

the fourth president of Israel and was followed by Yitzhak Navon, his former adjutant in the Haganah.

In 1978, Ephraim Katzir returned to his scientific activities at the Weizmann Institute in Rehovot and Tel Aviv University. He had many students who were inspired by his lectures and his scientific work. He passed away on May 30, 2009.

C. Ernst David Bergmann, Father of the *Israeli Nuclear Program*

E.D. Bergmann (Picture 101) was born in Germany in 1903 and received his doctorate in medicine and chemistry from the University of Berlin. When the Nazi party took over, he moved to the Institute of Pharmodynamics at the University of Amsterdam (1933–1934). In 1934, he was invited by Chaim Weizmann to join the Sieff Institute in Rehovot. After moving to Rehovot, Bergmann became a member of the Technological-Chemical Commission of Taas and in 1937 developed methods for the production of explosives and tear gas.

At the beginning of World War II, he worked for a short time in France (before its occupation by Germany) and then moved to England and finally to the United States, where he joined Chaim Weizmann and worked with him in several laboratories. On February 10, 1948, Bergmann returned to Rehovot and was appointed scientific director of the Weizmann Institute, which had just opened. Soon after his arrival, he met with Ben-Gurion and joined the Scientific Council, which dealt with the research and development of security problems. In February of 1948, Ben-Gurion appointed him chairperson of the Scientific Council, with Aharon Katchalsky as secretary and Shlomo Gur as administration officer.

In August of 1948, Prof. Yohanan Ratner was sent to the Soviet Union, and Bergmann was appointed chairperson of the Scientific Department of the Ministry of Defense (118).

Bergmann established close contact with Ben-Gurion based on mutual respect. Ben-Gurion planned to appoint Bergmann commander of HEMED and to give him a high military rank. On July 15, 1948, Ben-Gurion wrote:

> I have asked the chief of staff to appoint you as the commander of HEMED and to bestow upon you a rank which will be determined by him. In addition I appoint you counselor to the minister of defense. I wish you much success in your future work, which is not unfamiliar to you. This appointment is effective from today, July 15, 1951 (119).

Bergmann refused to receive a military rank, saying, "If I travel abroad to obtain information, I prefer to appear as a civilian rather than an officer" (119).

Picture 101. Ernst David Bergmann

In 1951, Bergmann suggested that the Scientific Department be transferred from the Army to a new branch of the Ministry of Defense (120). One year later, Bergmann formed the

Israel Atomic Energy Commission (121). Ernst David Bergmann passed away on April 6, 1975. The site of Rafael, near Haifa, was subsequently named the David Institute to memorialize his contributions.

Felix Bergmann, Ernst's brother, was also active in the research and development of military weapons. During the 1940s, Felix began the production of explosives at the Sieff Institute in Rehovot. After the War of Independence, Felix moved to Jerusalem and served as a professor of pharmacology at The Hebrew University.

D. Shlomo Gur (Grezovsky), Commander of HEMED (Lt. Colonel) following Ephraim Katzir

Gur was born in 1913 in Uman (Ukraine). After the Bolshevik Revolution, he escaped to Romania and in 1913 sailed to Haifa. Following his arrival, he worked as a farmer in Mikveh Israel and in 1930 became one of the founders of Kibbutz Nir David (also called Tel Amal). During the riots of 1936–1939, Gur, who was a member of the kibbutz, invented the "Wall and Tower" strategy, which facilitated the formation of new settlements in hostile areas. The method was based on the transfer and construction of prefabricated towers and walls. In 1938, he helped David Hacohen to construct barbed wire fences on the northern border near Lebanon. From then on, he was regarded as an "activist."

In 1945, Gur began his studies on water irrigation problems in the United States. At that time he was interested in starting a national watering system, which was planned by the Jewish Agency in Palestine. On August 18 1947, he returned to Israel and resumed his activities in the Haganah (122). He was asked to report on the quantities of arms and ammunition that belonged to the Haganah. Contrary to the speculation that the

Haganah had significant amounts of military supplies, his findings were disappointing (122).

In October 1947, Gur was appointed director of "non-
scientific matters" of the recently established Scientific Council.
Gur was not appreciated by his associates as he disagreed
with them and was not familiar with scientific research (123).
Because of these disagreements and the criticism of his
associates. Some of them left their job (124). In the 1950s, Gur
had a conflict with Motta Gur, the chief of staff, and Ernst
Bergmann sent him a note that read, "I was asked by the chief
of staff to inform you that you can take a leave of absence and
go wherever you want" (34).

E. Alex Keynan, Commander of HEMED B

Alex Keynan (Picture 102) was born in 1921 in Kiev
(Ukraine). His family moved to Tel Aviv and Keynan studied at
Herzliya High School (88). At the age of fifteen, he joined the
Haganah and received military training. After graduating from
high school, he began his studies at The Hebrew University.
The following year, he was sent to an officers' course organized
by the Haganah in Kibbutz Kfar Menachem. He claimed that
the conditions and training were difficult, especially when the
British Police detected them and they had to escape to Mount
Carmel to finish their training. Upon completing the course, he
returned to Jerusalem and was ordered to report to Ephraim
Katzir, who was a commander of a Hish company at the time.
Katzir appointed him as his adjutant. In addition to this assignment, Keynan was asked to recruit new members for the Haganah. Later, he was asked by Ben-Menachem, who was the director of the Animal House at The Hebrew University, whether
he would be willing to join the Haganah's intelligence service.
Keynan agreed and served under Miriam Ben-Aharon. Moshe
Shilo, a microbiologist, was in charge of the storage of illegal

weapons in Jerusalem. Yitzhak Navon and Morris Sasson were in charge of the Arab Department. Malka, Keynan's wife, was active in intelligence and formed contacts with foreign agents.

Picture 102. Alex Keynan

Keynan studied microbiology at The Hebrew University and in 1945 received his MSc degree. In 1950 he completed his doctorate under the guidance of Prof. Manfred Ashner. In 1952, Keynan was appointed scientific director of the Israel Institute for Biological Research in Ness Ziona and in 1963 became deputy chairperson of the National Council of Research and Development of the State of Israel. From 1979 until 1990, he was the chairperson of the Research and Development Department of The Hebrew University and initiated collaboration with different countries and universities, including Egypt. From 1979 to 1984, he was a visiting professor at various universities and a counselor for research and development of the United Nations and the World Health Organization. From 1990 he was advisor to the president of The Hebrew University and the president of the Israel Academy of Science and Humanities. Alex Keynan passed away on May 7, 2012.

F. Israel Dostrovsky, Commander of HEMED C

Dostrovsky (Picture 103) was born in Odessa in 1918 and one year later his family immigrated to Palestine and settled in Jerusalem. He studied at Rehavia High School and joined the Haganah. When he graduated high school in 1935, he started his studies on Mount Scopus and was responsible for the communication services of the Haganah. When the Israeli Army was formed, he continued his activity in the Communication Corps for over fifty years. In 1936, Dostrovsky commenced his studies at the University College in London and specialized in physical chemistry in the laboratories of Edward Hughes and Christopher Ingold. In 1943, Dostrovsky obtained his PhD in physical chemistry and received an academic appointment at the University of London.

Picture 103. Israel Dostrovsky

On April 1, 1948, Dostrovsky returned to Israel and was appointed by Ben-Gurion to serve as commander of HEMED C. He was assisted by the Army and established his headquarters at the "Hill" (now called the Ayalon Institute). From there, he organized geological expeditions. In addition he worked at the Weizmann Institute, where he produced "heavy water" (water enriched with heavy oxygen isotopes). Dostrovsky headed the Atomic Energy Commission between 1966 and 1971, a period that included the outbreak of the Six-Day War in 1967. He was the fifth president of the Weizmann Institute. Later, he was a leading figure in a military intelligence unit that formed the basis for scientific activities in the Ministry of Defense. He was also active in planning the nuclear research in the Dimona and Soreq centers. He was among those who supported the development of Israel's nuclear program, and he became the general manager of the Atomic Energy Commission. Dostrovsky was an Israel Prize laureate for exact sciences (physics, chemistry, mathematics) and also won many prizes in the field of physical chemistry, a field in which he was a leading figure. He passed away on September 28, 2010, at the age of ninety-two and was buried in a family plot in Kibbutz Maoz Haim in the Beit She'an Valley, where he was one of the founding members.

G. Yohanan (Jenka) Ratner, HEMED Chief Engineer

Ratner (Picture 104) was born in 1909 in Switzerland, where his parents studied medicine. After they completed their studies, the family returned to the Soviet Union. When Jenka was nine years old, his mother passed away and he joined his father, who became a military physician, and traveled all over the country. At the age of thirteen, Ratner immigrated to Palestine with his grandfather, Prof. Iliov, who founded the faculty of chemistry at the Technion in Haifa. During his work at the Technion, Iliov joined the Haganah and upgraded the Molotov cocktail, which was also named after him.

In 1931, Ratner completed his civil engineering studies at the Technion and found a position at the Iraq Petroleum Company (IPC). He was an adventurer and traveled throughout Asia on his motorcycle. In 1938, he joined the Haganah and developed land mines and explosives. In 1942, he was recruited by the British Army and placed by the Admiralty on the docks of Portsmouth, where he developed weaponry against German submarines. In 1947, he was asked to return to Israel and only after pretending to be seriously ill received permission from the Admiralty to leave his position. Because of this subterfuge, he suspected he might have been followed.

Picture 104. Jenka Ratner, chief engineer of HEMED

After arriving in Israel, Ratner received a desk in the so-called "Studio" at 6 Frug Street in Tel Aviv. In October of 1947, the Scientific Department was formed by the Haganah and Ratner became one of its leading members (125). On May 5, 1948, Ratner reported that prior to the establishment of the State, the following weapons were studied and some of them produced (126):

• Fuses for detonation
• Anti-personnel mines

- Anti-vehicle mines
- PIAT
- Flame throwers
- Anti-tank rifles
- Six-inch mortars
- Air bombs

Under Ratner's guidance, PIAT weapons were manufactured. They fulfilled important roles in the battles of Safed and Jerusalem. When HEMED was formed, Ratner was appointed chief engineer. There he developed various weapons, including the six-inch mortar. Subsequently he moved to Rafael with the rank of colonel. From 1969 to 1978 he was a senior advisor at Rafael. He passed away on March 25, 1979, having led a productive and successful life.

H. Shneor Lipson

Lipson (Picture 105) was born on March 18, 1914, in Tel Aviv. He studied at Herzliya High School and together with his classmates founded a new kibbutz in the Jezreel Valley. There he taught life sciences at the local school. In 1942, Lipson joined the Palmach and after one year of service asked for permission to study physics and chemistry at The Hebrew University.

After completing his studies, he returned to his kibbutz and resumed his teaching activities. When the War of Independence broke out he was asked by Aharon Katchalsky to join the physicists who worked at the Weizmann Institute, Subsequently, he was appointed deputy commander of HEMED. After the war, when Aharon Katchalsky invited him to join the newly established Deartment of Polymer Department at the Weizmann Institute, Lipson agreed, but he also continued his studies at The Hebrew University and in 1954 completed his doctorate.

Picture 105. Shneor Lipson

Following several years of research at the universities of Cornell and Harvard, Lipson returned to Rehovot and introduced new approaches to the study of polymers. From 1963 to 1967, he was the scientific director of the Weizmann Institute and from 1972 to 1978 headed the faculty of chemistry of the Weizmann Institute. In 1970, he was asked by Yigal Allon, who was then the minister of education, to create an open university. When this university was finally opened, he served as its rector. Lipson was a respected scientist who received many prizes. He passed away on January 22, 2001.

CHAPTER 17:

THE CONTRIBUTION OF HEMED
TO THE SECURITY OF ISRAEL

After the end of the War of Independence, Israeli leaders wondered whether young Israeli scientists and engineers had contributed much to the security of the State of Israel, as suggested by Ben-Gurion. The discussions can be divided into the two following parts: the contribution to successes during the War of Independence and the contribution to the future development of science in the country.

A. Contribution to Successes During the War of Independence

At the end of 1947, the leaders of the Jewish Agency were surprised to find out that the quantities of arms and ammunition in the hands of the Haganah were so limited. The embargo imposed by Western countries prevented the purchase of weapons from foreign sources. Fortunately, the Haganah set up an armaments industry, which produced hand grenades, submachine guns, and bullets. These were not enough to face invading Arab armies, which were well equipped. It was therefore decided that all available manpower should be recruited to improve the existing industry and perhaps also to develop new weapons.

HEMED was commissioned to accomplish these tasks. The armament industry started the production of weapons designed by HEMED scientists.

Munya Mardor, one of the leaders of Rafael, asked Ephraim Katzir to join him there. On May 1, 1960, Mardor received the following message from Ephraim Katzir (127):

Dear Munya,

I thank you very much for your friendly letter of April 5, 1960. It is a real privilege to return to Rafael, to join you, and to work with the associates who are under your command. During the War of Independence, I was one of the leaders of HEMED and planned its activities. I am therefore delighted to find out that the seeds I planted grew into a prosperous, many-branched tree.

When Ephraim Katzir was asked whether HEMED had contributed much to the security of the State of Israel and the efforts to build up a new country, he stated the following:

Jenka Ratner presented to me the following details, which comprise an impressive list of weapons produced by the armament industry as a result of HEMED's R&D.

• PIAT launchers 1,800
• PIAT shells 77,000
• Jumping land mines 11,000
• Manual land mines 100,000 [62]

It is possible that Ratner exaggerated the figures in his statement, since in March of 1948 he reported that by that date the armament industry had produced the following weapons (28):

• Jumping land mines 60,000
• Manual land mines 60,000

- Heavy six-inch mortars 50
- Heavy six-inch mortar shells 1,000
- M-2 launchers 10
- M-2 launcher shells 500

These numbers are very impressive and do not include weapons produced in the besieged city of Jerusalem.

It is very difficult to speculate what the fate of besieged Jerusalem would have been without the contribution of HEMED and local industry. One has to remember that all the roads leading to Jerusalem were blocked. The steadfast devotion of "crazy" Aharon Katchalsky and Elik Sochazewer, who began their activities at The Hebrew University on Mount Scopus, played an extremely important role in the survival of the besieged city during those critical days (128).

The joint efforts of HEMED scientists and the armament industry produced weapons and ammunition. Thus, cheddite, which was the only explosive produced in Jerusalem, was used to produce mines and hand grenades. Detonators were also manufactured in primitive workshops. Hollow-charged weapons saved Jerusalem. One of them was the *Conus*, which was supposed to break through the walls of the Old City. PIAT launchers and shells, the "Davidka," and six-inch mortars permitted the defense of Jerusalem and stopped attacks by the Arab Legion and "irregular forces," which consisted of armed Palestinian villagers who did not belong to the regular armies.

Zvi Pelach described the joint activities of HEMED and the industries as follows (34):

> The young scientists of HEMED were innovative in their outlooks and produced weapons that were supposed to be impossible to produce. It is very likely that because they were so young and had limited knowledge, they dared to do things that established scientists considered

impossible. If you lack knowledge, you invent new concepts and you lead to breakthroughs. Sometimes, knowing too much is a disadvantage (34)!

Aviv Feldbrovsky joined HEMED in March 1948 and produced incendiary weapons. Later he became scientific director of Base No. 1 and, therefore, his evaluations are of great importance. He stated:

> Indeed, we were very young and always engaged in emergency activities. We never had a quiet moment. We were constantly approached by military commanders who asked us to solve problems. HEMED was regarded as a "wizard." If they did not know what to do by using conventional methods, they said, "Let us go to the 'boys.' Perhaps they will have new ideas and open new avenues" (129).

Close communications existed between HEMED and the various IDF units. The Air Force, the Navy, and ground forces alike were very active in this respect. The operation units of HEMED transmitted the results of laboratory research to the battlefield. HEMED scientists were also instructors at the officers' academy and introduced new disciplines into military units.

1. Navy

The Mediterranean Sea is the western border of the State of Israel. This is a relatively long border and it was difficult to protect the country with the primitive Israeli Navy established in 1947–1948. The Haganah and later the IDF planned to develop a torpedo or a "long-range marine missile" that could be used at sea.

Uzi Sharon was a pioneer in the development of a propelled weapon. As early as 1947, he was asked to design a torpedo to damage British destroyers that were taking part in expelling "illegal" Jewish immigrants." Later, Jenka Ratner, Yedidia Shamir, and Jonathan Maas joined Uzi Sharon and designed remote-controlled explosive boats.

According to Asher Asher, Israel Pelach developed an infrared lamp to illuminate targets at night (42). An Egyptian battleship, *The King Farouk*, anchored near Gaza, and the Israeli Navy planned to attack it with a torpedo. Yohai Ben-Nun (who in the 1960s became commander of Israel's naval forces as a rear admiral) volunteered to fire the torpedo. He was certain that the Egyptian vessel would be hit and that its sailors would jump overboard. If this happened, how could he be selected and rescued by our rescue team? HEMED scientists designed helmets with infrared lamps, which Ben-Nun and his associate wore. The rescue team could detect the light and select them from the swimming Egyptian sailors. This is an excellent example that demonstrates that when HEMED was asked to solve a critical problem, it found a creative solution.

Another problem faced the Israeli Navy. An Egyptian ship loaded with weapons was supposed to sail from Italy to Egypt. Israeli intelligence planned to destroy the ship by attaching a magnetic limpet mine to its bottom. We were asked to design a fuse that would initiate an explosion when the ship was on the high sea far from port. At that time we did not have remote communication tools with which to initiate the explosion. A time bomb was also ruled out, as we did not have any information concerning the sailing time. I discussed the matter with Berdichevsky, a young mechanical engineer, and finally found a solution. A fuse would be attached to a propeller, which would not rotate when the ship was anchored. Upon sailing, the propeller would rotate and after a predetermined number of rotations, it would ignite the detonator, which would activate the explosives in the mine. I am not certain whether it was used to destroy the specific Egyptian vessel in question, but I was informed by

Yehuda Venezia, a pioneer of the Palmach, that this device was brought to his attention.

2. Air Force

At the beginning of the War of Independence, the Air Force had only primitive Piper and Dakota aircraft. We had neither aerial bombs to be dropped from aircraft, nor flares to operate at night. When planes were used during the attack on Nebi Daniel, Amos Chorev and Yehuda Venezia dropped simple bombs that consisted of iron pipes filled with explosives from a Piper aircraft. This situation did not change significantly when American B-17 planes and Czechoslovakian Messerschmitt aircraft arrived. HEMED was therefore asked to supply the Israeli Air Force with suitable aerial bombs. Incendiary bombs containing napalm and thermites were designed and manufactured. They were dropped on the airport of El-Arish and on fortifications of the Fallujah Pocket. HEMED was also asked to produce flares so the Air Force could operate at night. The Israeli Air Force recognized the potential of HEMED and appointed Shaike Yarkoni liaison officer to connect HEMED with the Israeli Air Force.

3. Ground Forces

Ground forces consisted of infantry and armor corps. They all were aided by HEMED scientists and operation units. Considerable effort was invested in the development of hollow charges for guns and ammunition. This led to the design of the famous *Conus*, which was used in the battle for the Old City. The development of flame throwers was also one of the major projects studied by HEMED scientists. They developed the ignition component and the mechanical components of this weapon.

The close collaboration of physicists with Jenka Ratner led to the production of the M-2 cannon and the six-inch mortar. HEMED scientists were also asked to design and develop fuses for artillery shells. Smoke and incendiary hand grenades and mortar shells were designed and used in battle during the day and at night. Operation units also instructed field units on the use of the new weapons developed by HEMED. These units played a central role in exploring unknown areas and provided essential information to the industry and research in the State of Israel.

4. Military Rabbinate

Rabbi Shlomo Goren, chief rabbi of the IDF, heard about HEMED and asked its scientists to develop an illumination system that could be used during the celebration of the thirty-third day of the Counting of the Omer, Lag B'Omer.[32] HEMED pyrotechnical scientists constructed a flare system that shed light that could be seen all over the Galilee.

B. Contribution to the Future Development of Science in the Country

In 1951, a number of scientists and military personnel wondered whether the activities of HEMED should be continued. In order to solve the dilemma, Shlomo Gur organized an impressive display of armaments and inventions that were the fruits of HEMED's activities. Yigael Yadin, who headed a special committee, expressed his enthusiasm concerning the display and was highly impressed by HEMED's achievements. He stated that HEMED's research should be continued. In 1952, Shlomo Gur met with Ben-Gurion and suggested that HEMED should be converted into a civilian unit and become a research and planning branch of the Ministry of Defense.

---

32 Lag B'Omer is a Jewish holiday celebrated on the thirty-third day of the Counting of the Omer, which occurs on the eighteenth day of the Hebrew month of Iyar. Well-known customs and practices on Lag B'Omer include the lighting of bonfires on Mount Meron near Safed in the Galilee.

In addition to the previous aspects of research, it was decided to develop missiles that could be used by aircraft to fire at ground or naval targets. It was argued that these missiles would add a new dimension to naval battles. Jonathan Maas and Phidia Piatly, who had started to develop the Angel missile, were in charge of this research and development (130).

Even if some people questioned the importance of HEMED during the War of Independence, there was no doubt that it trained a new generation of scientists and engineers who later fulfilled central functions in the scientific community of the newly created State of Israel. Igal Talmi was correct in stating that HEMED was the infant from which Israeli science developed (55). Universities and research institutes in Israel were manned by scientists who started their research in HEMED. HEMED B was converted into the Israel Institute for Biological Research in Ness Ziona. HEMED physicists joined the Weizmann Institute and formed the Department of Nuclear Physics from which the Atomic Energy Commission developed. Chemists and mechanical engineers who started their research at HEMED continued their activities at Rafael and produced missiles that were sold for $2 billion. Thanks to their devotion, Rafael became a world leader in research and development. All of this was the result of the vision of David Ben-Gurion, the devotion of Aharon and Ephraim Katzir, the steadfast support of E.D. Bergmann, and the praiseworthy activity of Shlomo Gur. The vitally important contributions of Jenka Ratner and Elik Sochazewer should also be acknowledged.

CHAPTER 18:

WHAT HAPPENED AFTER HEMED?

Highly qualified scientists ("HEMED graduates") continued their research at Rafael and the Ministry of Defense. Zvi Pelach and Moshe (Moja) Epstein are good examples. Here are some of the stories of other scientists, told in their own their own words (all translated from the Hebrew):

A. Gideon Peleg (Pavlovic)

I joined HEMED on May 19, 1948, and took part in a course on mining and demolition given to members of the Palmach by Zvi Pelach. I learned how to attach detonators to a detonation cord and how to use explosives. I was then interviewed by Alon Feldman[-Radler-Talmi] and Ernst Fischer and asked to join the incendiary group. There I learned how to produce incendiary bombs and grenades that contained white phosphorus, solid fuel, and napalm. Izzy Kahana was the head of our group, but when his leg was injured during one of the experiments, he was discharged from the Army. I replaced him and worked with two dear friends under my supervision: Shmaya Ben-

Moshe (who was later killed in a car accident) and the late Edmond Uziel.

Our contact was with the Air Force, who asked us to prepare air bombs containing liquid fuel, which consisted of petrol to which natural rubber or crepe rubber were added. Later, we also used napalm, which was imported and synthesized by us. The fuel was poured into containers usually used as reserve fuel tanks for airplanes. Shmaya Ben-Moshe prepared incendiary bombs that contained solid fuel based on aluminum powder, gypsum, and magnesium.

In HEMED, no orders were given; officers and privates were treated equally and the atmosphere was very friendly. There was no difference between the soldiers who guarded the gates and the scientists who worked on research and development. I know that one of the guards became a pilot and a colonel in the Air Force, while another one had a top position in the Ministry of Foreign Affairs.

In 1951, I was sent to France to study chemical engineering. When I returned, HEMED did not exist anymore and Rafael had been formed.

I was wounded. We used white phosphorus as a source for smoke screens and for anti-personnel hand grenades. We all knew that white phosphorus was very sensitive and ignited when exposed to air. It was very difficult to work with this chemical and we developed an automatic system to fill the hand grenades. I had a protective mask shielding my face, and yet splinters of phosphorus hit my face. I knew that copper sulfate could neutralize white phosphorus and applied it immediately. The nurse, Josephine, treated me and sent me to a hospital in Jaffa. Luckily no scars were left on my face (70).

B. Yehuda Venezia

Yehuda Venezia was born in Jaffa in 1921 to parents who emigrated from Thessaloniki. They opened a hardware store in Jaffa and helped with the integration of new immigrants who came from Greece. As a result of riots in Jaffa, the family moved to Tel Aviv. Venezia studied at high schools in Tel Aviv and joined the "Civil Haganah," which was the right wing of the Haganah. He started to study architecture at the Technion in Haifa, but after two years he decided to enlist either in the British forces or the Palmach. He encountered difficulties in becoming a member of the Palmach because of his "rightist past." Finally, he succeeded and even completed a platoon commanders' course. In 1946, he returned to Tel Aviv and joined his father in the family business.

In November of 1947, Venezia was asked by Haim Singer to join a course of mining and demolition together with Netiva Ben-Yehuda. Thus, he became one of the demolition experts of the Palmach. His first assignment was to plant mines near the border with Syria to prevent the invasion of Syrian forces. At that time he had his first contact with HEMED. He became part of the group at Frug Street and manufactured land and anti-tank mines. Jenka Ratner and Aharon Donagi supplied him with explosives (mainly cheddite) and PIAT weaponry. Venezia maintained his contacts with HEMED in the 1950s when he was active in security missions (16).

C. Aviv Peleg (Feldbrovsky)

Feldbrovsky worked in Ramat Gan in a factory that produced orange juice. He was asked by Aharon Katzir and Bergmann to join the Scientific Department of the Haganah and to act as secretary of the meetings. In February or March of 1948, he was officially recruited by HEMED and became a member of the incendiary group that worked at the "Grey House."

Here is his story:

> As far as I can remember, I worked with the scientists of the incendiary group. Later the subjects of my research were solid fuels and napalm. Together with my girlfriend Shula (headquarters secretary), who became my wife, we constructed the first 30-kilogram napalm bombs. I was told that these bombs were used during the attack on El-Arish. We also constructed barrel bombs, which contained 100 kilograms of napalm and two incendiary grenades. When the barrel was dropped from an airplane, it was crushed, the fuel spread, and the grenades ignited it.
>
> We were young and educated in different disciplines. We shared one important common dominator, a spirit of devotion, volunteering and sincere cooperation. We never had a dull moment and were always in a state of emergency (129).

Feldbrovsky served in Base No. 1 and in the 1950s was appointed scientific director of the base (130). Zvi Pelach replaced Feldbrovsky when he was sent to the United Kingdom to study the properties of plastic ware.

D. Uriel Bachrach

Even after completing my military service, I continued my association with the defense administration. As a civilian, I was asked to solve a challenging problem. Colonel Shmuel Albeck wrote in his book *Sand and Arms* (131) that he was appointed to recover the bodies of missing Israeli soldiers who were killed during the Yom Kippur War. About five hundred soldiers who fought at the "Chinese Farm" and the fortifications near the Suez Canal died in action and their bodies were not found. As the Sinai Peninsula had to be given back to Egypt in 1973, their bodies had to be found.

Albeck wrote in his book:

> We searched for the bodies of the missing soldiers for one month without positive results. I came to the conclusion that we had to use a different approach and decided to consult with scientists on the matter. I decided to contact the best scientists in our country and ask them to find a solution to the problem.
>
> I have a friend, Uriel Bachrach, whom I knew from my childhood in Petach Tikvah. He was a microbiologist at The Hebrew University. I called him and told him, "Uriel, I have a problem and I do not know how to solve it. At noon tomorrow a plane will be waiting for you at Ben Gurion Airport to take you to Rephidim Airport in the Sinai Peninsula. You have to know that we will not leave Rephidim unless we solve our problem" (131).

I flew to the Sinai Peninsula the following morning with high-ranking police officers, including Inspector Kaplan, the head of Criminal Investigation Department, and his deputy Yossi Almog. Shmuel Albeck took us to the "Chinese Farm" and the fortifications near the Suez Canal and we gathered and discussed possible solutions. The police officers suggested we take air samples and analyze them by gas chromatography to detect signs of putrefaction. Another suggestion was to use air photography to detect spots in which vegetation was more abundant. These suggestions were rejected.

Albeck recalls:

> Then Uriel offered two suggestions. In Vietnam American forces faced the problem of detecting tunnels in which Vietcong fighters were hiding. They used insects and flies that could sense the proximity of human flesh and point to the hiding places (131).

The idea was to find these insects and flies, confine them in small boxes, and watch their movements and behavior. This suggestion was not accepted. Albeck reports in his book:

> During the discussions, Uriel remarked, "I have seen wild dogs looking for prey in the wilderness, and when they smell rotten flesh they start digging. I believe that we can use dogs to find the missing bodies. Perhaps we should capture some of those wild dogs and use them for our purpose" (131).

Albeck and the police officers found this idea attractive, and Inspector Kaplan contacted Scotland Yard officers in London and requested their help. He was told that the British Police had dogs that were trained to smell and find corpses. Albeck contacted Hadar Kimchi, our military attaché in London, and asked him to find out about these dogs. Two days later, he informed Albeck that the British Police had four dogs and with the permission of the United Nations and the Egyptian army, Scotland Yard would agree to send the dogs to the Sinai Peninsula. There was another condition: British policemen would accompany the dogs. The Egyptian general Mahjub did not agree to British policemen entering the Sinai Peninsula. Albeck told Mahjub, "If you do not agree, we will stop shipments of food and water to the besieged Third Army in the Sinai Peninsula." General Mahjub finally agreed, and the dogs arrived with their policemen trainers. Together with representatives of the Military Rabbinate we found the bodies of 490 missing soldiers. Dentists helped to identify the bodies, as DNA analyses were not available in those days.

Here we see an example of how cooperation between devoted scientists and military personnel led to positive results. It is obvious that neither body could have solved the problem on its own. Thanks to this joint activity, almost all of the bodies of the five hundred missing soldiers were retrieved and brought back to Israel for burial.

REFERENCES

1. A meeting sponsored by The Israel Academy of Science and Humanities on April 10, 2006. Recorded by B. Ory

2. דרור צ., **הראל - הקרב על ירושלים**, הוצאת הקיבוץ המאוחד, עמ' 64 (2006)

3. דרור צ., **הראל - הקרב על ירושלים**, הוצאת הקיבוץ המאוחד, עמ' 289 (2006)

4. יוני הקשר של חיל הקשר, הוצאת מערכות (1953)

5. אריאלי י., **גדנ"ע ירושלים בתש"ח**, משרד הביטחון - ההוצאה לאור, עמ' 37 (2003)

6. אריאלי י., **גדנ"ע ירושלים בתש"ח**, משרד הביטחון - ההוצאה לאור, עמ' 38 (2003)

7. שולוב א., **מגיני ההר**, האוניברסיטה העברית, חוברת ב' כרך 14, ירושלים עמ' 57 (תשכ"ט)

8. A letter written by A. Katchalsky on March 28, 1948

9. גור ש., תיק עדויות (ת.ע.) חמ"ד מס. 1/2, עמ' 10, נלקח מ- איזנפלד א. **שורשי חיל המדע (חמ"ד) בארגון ההגנה**, אוניברסיטת תל-אביב, עמ' 11 (1984)

10. ברגמן א.ד., מכתב לחיים ויצמן מיום 31 למאי, נלקח מ- איזנפלד א. **שורשי חיל המדע (חמ"ד) בארגון ההגנה**, אוניברסיטת תל-אביב, עמ' 12 (1984)

11. קציר אפרים. בהקדמה לספרו של מרדור מ., **רפא"ל: בנתיבי המחקר והפיתוח לביטחון ישראל**, משרד הביטחון, עמ' 11 (1981)

12. An interview with A. Chorev on February 5 (2006)

13. An interview with G. Blauer on September 18 (2005)

14. An interview with Y. Navon on December 30 (2005)

15. דרור צ., **הראל - הקרב על ירושלים,** הוצאת הקיבוץ המאוחד, עמ' 68 (2006)

16. An interview with Y. Venezia on January 5 (2006)

17. נרקיס ע., **חייל של ירושלים,** משרד הביטחון - ההוצאה לאור, עמ' 80 (1991)

18. בן- גוריון ד., ישיבה שביעית של הכנסת הראשונה

19. בן- גוריון ד., האסיפה הכללית הראשונה של האקדמיה למדעים ביום 23 כפברואר (1960)

20. קציר א., האסיפה הכללית הראשונה של האקדמיה למדעים ביום 23 בפברואר (1960)

21. בן- גוריון ד., **בהילחם עם,** הוצאת עם עובד, עמ' 236 (1950)

22. רטנר י., **חיי ואני,** הוצאת שוקן, עמ' 338 (1978)

23. מרדור מ., **רפא"ל: בנתיבי המחקר והפיתוח לביטחון ישראל,** משרד הביטחון - ההוצאה לאור, עמ' 72 (1981)

24. קצ'לסקי א., ליבוביץ י., בריל מ., **חידושי המדע והמלחמה,** הוצאת רימון (1943)

25. N. Balchin, The Small Back Room. Pan Books, Ltd., London (1947)

26. ארד נ., דו"ח מרס (1977)

27. www.global-report.net/text/a.php?t=um&id=80&c=um

28. An interview with R. Eshel on February 21 (2006)

29. מרדור מ., **רפא"ל: בנתיבי המחקר והפיתוח לביטחון ישראל,** משרד הביטחון - ההוצאה לאור, עמ' 73 (1981)

30. An interview with M. Zarchi on January 25 (2006)

31. איזנפלד א., **שורשי חיל המדע (חמ"ד) בארגון ההגנה,** אוניברסיטת תל- אביב, עמ' 43 (1984)

32. An interview with N. Sharon on August 24 (2005)

33. An interview with S. - Gallily on September 5 (2005)

34. A report by Z. Pelach, November 5 (1981)

35. A report by E. Katzir, April 30 (1982)

36. An interview with Y. Ben-Ari on March 19 (2006)

37. A report given by M. Pikarsky on April 10 (2006)

38. An interview with Z. Tzur on August 16 (2006)

39. בן- גוריון ד., **יומן המלחמה** מיום 18 במרס (1948)

40. פקודת מטכ״ל אג״א מיום 19 למרס (1948)

41. An interview with U. Littauer on August 8 (2005)

42. A report given by A. Asher on November 9 (1981)

43. www.nrg.co.il/online/1/ART/955/943.html-74k

44. An interview with A. Kedem on November 26 (2005)

45. An interview with B. Tidhar on March 2 (2006)

46. An interview with M. Bar-Ilan on December 15 (2006)

47. H. Eisenberg Selected Topics in the History of Biochemistry: Personal Recollection (Semenza G. and Jaeniche R. eds.) Chapter 8 p. 265 (1990)

48. An interview with I. Miller on August 8 (2006)

49. An interview with E. Kaufmann on August 26 (2005)

50. An interview with O. Kedem on October 26 (2005)

51. An interview with A. Damiel (Schweiger) on January 25 (2006)

52. עברון י., **התעשייה הביטחונית בישראל**, משרד הביטחון - ההוצאה לאור, עמ׳ 129 (1980)

53. לפידות י., **על חומותיך**, משרד הביטחון - ההוצאה לאור, עמ׳ 306 (1992)

54. יכין ע., **סיפורו של לוחם חרות ישראל**, הוצאת יאיר, תל-אביב עמ׳ 312 (1993)

55. An interview with I. Talmi on January 8 (2006)

56. A report by A. Chorev on February 5 (2006)

57. עברון י., **התעשייה הביטחונית בישראל**, משרד הביטחון - ההוצאה לאור עמ׳ 128 (1980)

58. Archives of I.D.F

59. An interview with M. Epstein on May 28 (2006)

60. יקותיאלי ג., **ימי חמד**, בהוצאת היחידה לפעולות נוער, מכון ויצמן למדע, רחובות, עמ' 22 (1996)

61. An interview with G. Goldring on January 2 (2006)

62. A Report by E. Katzir on August 10 (2006)

63. כהן א., **ישראל והפצצה**, הוצאת שוקן ירושלים, עמ' 41 (2000)

64. דונגי א., ארכיון ההגנה, עדות אהרונצ'יק דונגי מיום 21.1.51. איזנפלד א. **שורשי חיל המדע (חמ"ד) בארגון ההגנה**, אוניברסיטת תל-אביב, עמ' 14 (1984)

65. An interview with Y. Ben-Hanan on May 10 (2005)

66. לורך נ., **קורות מלחמת העצמאות**, מודן הוצאה לאור, תל-אביב, עמ' 326 (1998)

67. לורך נ., **קורות מלחמת העצמאות**, מודן הוצאה לאור, תל-אביב, עמ' 336 (1998)

68. לורך נ., **קורות מלחמת העצמאות**, מודן הוצאה לאור, תל-אביב, עמ' 555 (1998)

69. כהן י., **לאור היום ובמחשך**, הוצאת עמיקם, עמ' 190 (תשכ"ט)

70. A report by G. Pavlovic (Peleg) on November 5 (1998)

71. Cohen A. Israel and Chemical/Biological Weapons: History, Deterence, and Arms Control. The Nonproliferation Reviews/ Fall Winter, p.27 (2001)

72. כהן א., **הטאבו האחרון**, כנרת, זמורה-ביתן-מוציאים לאור, עמ' 267 (2005)

73. ליבוביץ-דר ש., בעיתון חדשות, 13 אוגוסט (1993)

74. g/e_research/profiles/egypt/3370.html http://www.nti.or

75. Cohen, A. The Rise of CB Weapons" The problem of Chemical and Biological Warfare. Stockholm International Peace Research Institute, Vol. 2. p. 319, Stockholm. Almquist and Wiskell, (1971)

76. FBIS-NES-98-320;11/17/98

77. Shoham D. Evolution of Chemical and Biological Weapons in Egypt. ACPR Policy Paper No. 46
http://www. acpr.org.il/publications/policy –papers/pp46-xs.html

78. כהן א., **הטאבו האחרון**, כנרת ,זמורה-ביתן-מוציאים לאור, עמ' 272 (2005)

79. לורך נ., **קורות מלחמת העצמאות**, מודן הוצאה לאור, תל-אביב, עמ' 190 (1989)

80. כהן א., **הטאבו האחרון**, כנרת ,זמורה-ביתן-מוציאים לאור, עמ' 270 (2005)

81. html http://www.plands.org/articles/10

82. כהן י., **לאור היום ובמחשך**, הוצאת עמיקם, עמ' 66 (תשכ"ט)

83. גורדון ת., **מרגלי גדעון**, הוצאת אור עם, עמ' 384 (1999)

84. כהן א., **הטאבו האחרון**, כנרת זמורה-ביתן-מוציאים לאור, עמ' 275 (2005)

85. http://www.iibr.gov/il

86. www.nrc.nl/w2/Lab/Ziona

87. J., Mager *Nature* **176**, 933, (1955)

88. An interview by A. Keynan on February 26 (2006)

89. An interview with I. Dostrovsky on August 8 (2005)

90. **מבצע עובדה**, עורכים אלחנן אורן ומאיר אביזוהר, המכון למורשת בן-גוריון, מדרשת שדה בוקר עמ' 7 (2002)

91. An interview with L. Macaresco on March 19 (2006)

92. כהן א., **ישראל והפצצה**, הוצאת שוקן תל-אביב, עמ' 55 (2000)

93. כהן א., **ישראל והפצצה**, הוצאת שוקן תל-אביב, עמ' 353 (2000)

94. כהן א., **ישראל והפצצה**, הוצאת שוקן תל-אביב עמ' 232 (2000)

95. שגב ת., בתכנית רשת ב' ברדיו ביום 12 לספטמבר (2005)

96. דרור צ., **הראל - הקרב על ירושלים**, הוצאת הקיבוץ המאוחד, עמ' 194 (2006)

97. לורך נ., **קורות מלחמת העצמאות**, מודן הוצאה לאור, תל-אביב, עמ' 222 (1989)

98. A classified report October 28 (1948)

99. An interview with Z. Shatil on January 5 (2006)

100. מרדור מ., **רפא"ל: בנתיבי המחקר והפיתוח לביטחון ישראל**, משרד הביטחון - ההוצאה לאור, עמ' 70 (1981)

101. עדותו של א., ברמן ת.ע חמ"ד מס. 17, עמ' 2. איזנפלד א. **שורשי חיל המדע (חמ"ד) בארגון ההגנה**, אוניברסיטת תל-אביב, עמ' 24 (1984)

102. עדותו של סוכצ'בר א., מיום 22.11.81, ת.ע. חמ"ד, עדות מס' 10, עמ' 4. איזנפלד א.. **שורשי חיל המדע (חמ"ד) בארגון ההגנה**, אוניברסיטת תל-אביב, עמ' 24 (1984)

103. A report by U. Bachrach on December 12 (1948)

104. בן- גוריון ד.. **יומן המלחמה 14** לינואר (1948)

105. A report by Y. Birk on April 10 (2006)

106. A report by U. Bachrach on September 19 (1948)

107. בן- גוריון ד.. יומן המלחמה עמ' 37, איזנפלד א.. **שורשי חיל המדע (חמ"ד) בארגון ההגנה**, אוניברסיטת תל-אביב, עמ' 52 (1984)

108. בלאס ש.. **מי מריבה ומעש**, הוצאת מסדה, עמ' 149 (1973)

109. גולדברג ס., ת. ע. חמ"ד, עדות מס' 29, עמ' 1, איזנפלד א.. **שורשי חיל המדע (חמ"ד) בארגון ההגנה**, אוניברסיטת תל-אביב, עמ' 83 (1984)

110. לורך נ.. **קורות מלחמת העצמאות**, מודן הוצאה לאור, תל-אביב, עמ' 595 (1989)

111. Wertheimer S.. Telephone talk July (2006)

112. איזנפלד א.. **שורשי חיל המדע (חמ"ד) בארגון ההגנה**, אוניברסיטת תל-אביב עמ' 20, (1984)

113. שרון ע.. **רפא"ל שלנו** גיליון 6 עמ' 1

114. אפשטיין מ.. גיליון 49, ידיעון רפא"ל

115. A report by M. Epstein April 10 (2006)

116. אשל ר.. **רפא"ל שלנו** גיליון 5 עמ' 26

117. עיתון דבר מיום 3 למאי (1960)

118. מרדור מ.. **רפא"ל: בנתיבי המחקר והפיתוח לביטחון ישראל**, משרד הביטחון - ההוצאה לאור, עמ' 75 (1981)

119 . מרדור מ.. **רפא"ל: בנתיבי המחקר והפיתוח לביטחון ישראל**, משרד הביטחון - ההוצאה לאור, עמ' 80 (1981)

120. מרדור מ.. **רפא"ל: בנתיבי המחקר והפיתוח לביטחון ישראל**, משרד הביטחון - ההוצאה לאור, עמ' 79 (1981)

121. כהן א.. **ישראל והפצצה**, הוצאת שוקן ירושלים, עמ' 34 (2000)

122. גור ש., ארכיון ההגנה, עדות שלמה גור משנת 1961, עמ' 1, איזנפלד א.. **שורשי חיל המדע (חמ"ד) בארגון ההגנה**, אוניברסיטת תל-אביב, עמ' 38 (1984)

123. ברמן א., ת. ע. חמ"ד, עדות מס' 17, עמ' 25, איזנפלד א., **שורשי חיל המדע (חמ"ד) בארגון ההגנה,** אוניברסיטת תל-אביב, עמ' 39 (1984)

124. פריי א., ת. ע. חמ"ד, עדות מס' 19, עמ' 3, איזנפלד א., **שורשי חיל המדע (חמ"ד) בארגון ההגנה,** אוניברסיטת תל-אביב, עמ' 39 (1984)

125. ידיעון רפא"ל, גיליון מס' 45

126. רטנר ז., עדות ג'נקה רטנר, ת.ע. חמ"ד עדות מס' 30 עמ' 2, איזנפלד א., **שורשי חיל המדע (חמ"ד) בארגון ההגנה,** אוניברסיטת תל-אביב עמ' 45 (1984)

127. מרדור מ., **רפא"ל: בנתיבי המחקר והפיתוח לביטחון ישראל,** משרד הביטחון - ההוצאה לאור, עמ' 199 (1981)

128. מרדור מ., **רפא"ל: בנתיבי המחקר והפיתוח לביטחון ישראל,** משרד הביטחון - ההוצאה לאור, עמ' 130 (1981)

129. A report by A. Fedbrovsky (Peleg) on November 5 (1998)

130. מרדור מ., **רפא"ל: בנתיבי המחקר והפיתוח לביטחון ישראל,** משרד הביטחון - ההוצאה לאור, עמ' 218 (1981)

131. אלבק ש., **חיל וחגור,** ביתן הוצאה לאור, תל-אביב, עמ' 226 (2003)

INDEX

www.ingramcontent.com/pod-product-compliance
Lightning Source LLC
Chambersburg PA
CBHW070346090426
42733CB00009B/1301